Gold
EXPERIENCE

A2
Key for Schools

Vocabulary
and Grammar
Workbook

Kathryn Alevizos

Contents

Enjoy yourself

VOCABULARY

1 **Match the hobbies with the pictures.**

> cooking   ~~dancing~~   drawing   fishing
> reading   singing

1   *dancing*

2 _____

3 _____

4 _____

5 _____

6 _____

2 **Complete the sentences with these words.**

> ~~cooking~~   dance   fishing   painting
> read   sing

1   Do you like ___*cooking*___ ?
Yes, I make really good cakes!

2   Do you always _____ a book before you go to bed?
Yes, every night.

3   Do your parents _____ ?
My mum does. She has a nice voice, but my dad doesn't.

4   Do you do _____ in your art class?
Yes and we do drawing.

5   Does Stephanie _____ ?
Yes, she does ballet.

6   Do you go _____ with your granddad in his boat?
Yes, and we cook what we catch when we get back.

3 **Choose the correct words.**

1   Martin loves *cook/cooking*. He makes great spaghetti bolognese.

2   Francesca goes *fishes/fishing* with her dad and brother every Sunday.

3   Caroline and Maisy *playing/play* in a rock band.

4   We usually *draw/drawing* animals or people in our art class.

5   They enjoy *read/reading* comics.

6   Do you like *sing/singing*?

7   I *cook/cooking* breakfast for my family every Saturday.

8   My brother's not very good at *paint/painting*.

4 Find and write four things you can play and three things you can watch.

c	h	f	y	t	r	f	r	e	d	n	f	i
l	o	k	j	u	h	g	f	d	e	e	s	k
i	o	m	u	s	l	i	g	v	n	g	f	e
l	b	h	p	o	o	n	u	n	e	i	t	u
k	v	y	i	u	f	t	i	u	n	i	b	d
e	h	u	a	t	t	e	t	e	n	d	v	d
m	k	o	n	o	n	e	a	n	g	l	i	o
t	u	i	o	n	f	d	r	c	n	f	m	x
v	n	t	r	e	e	r	i	g	d	i	n	t
o	e	m	b	t	i	g	e	e	a	l	b	i
t	n	c	h	e	s	s	n	o	n	m	l	n
e	v	i	n	u	s	k	o	n	e	k	e	k
d	i	p	o	j	d	e	o	g	r	e	a	s

Things you can play
1 _____piano_____
2 _____
3 _____
4 _____

Things you can watch
1 _____
2 _____
3 _____

5 Match the meanings (1–6) with the words (a–f).

1 the sounds you make playing instruments or singing
2 something that you post without an envelope
3 a small piece of paper you buy and stick onto a letter
4 an overnight visit to another person's home
5 you watch films in this building
6 a magazine with stories and pictures

a stamp
b comic
c cinema
d music
e postcard
f sleepover

6 Choose the correct verbs.

1 watch/_collect_ comics
2 play/go on a sleepover
3 watch/go a TV programme
4 watch/go to the cinema
5 listen/collect to music
6 play/watch the violin
7 watch/go shopping
8 listen/collect stamps

7 Match the sentences (1–8) with the sentences (A–H).

1 I love reading comics. _G_
2 Suzie and Rachel are good at football. _____
3 Ricky hates shopping. _____
4 I'm OK at drawing. _____
5 We don't like going to the cinema. _____
6 William's brilliant at chess. _____
7 My dad isn't good at singing. _____
8 Gina's got an amazing collection of postcards. _____

A He's got a terrible voice!
B He's always winning competitions.
C I prefer painting.
D They play for the school team.
E She's got 500!
F He thinks it's boring.
G My favourite is called *Demo*.
H We like watching DVDs at home.

8 Complete the text with the best answer, A, B or C, for each space.

My friends and I all 1) _____ different hobbies. I love singing and 2) _____ to my MP3 player. We all enjoy going to the 3) _____ together. Sometimes we watch a 4) _____ at someone's house. My friend Lucy 5) _____ the piano. She's really good. I play the 6) _____ . My brother doesn't like listening to me! He usually stays in his room and plays 7) _____ .

1 A take   (B) have   C make
2 A listening   B watching   C playing
3 A film   B sleepover   C cinema
4 A TV   B DVD   C computer games
5 A plays   B does   C makes
6 A shopping   B violin   C drawing
7 A MP3 player   B comics   C computer games

GRAMMAR
Present simple

1 Choose the correct words.

1 Oliver *plays/play* the guitar and the piano.
2 Melissa and Ruby *goes/go* shopping every Saturday.
3 He *don't/doesn't* have a hobby.
4 *Does/Do* they listen to music in the car?
5 We *doesn't/don't* like painting.
6 The children *watch/watches* TV after school.
7 She *take/takes* amazing photographs.
8 I *doesn't/don't* go to the cinema with my family.

2 Complete the letter with the present simple form of the verbs in brackets.

Hi, Tom

Summer camp 1) ____*is*____ (be) brilliant! We
2) _____ (do) lots of different activities here.
In the morning we play games. Sometimes I
3) _____ (play) chess and sometimes I do sport
outside. In the afternoon we do art and music. I
4) _____ (like) painting and drawing. My brother
5) _____ (enjoy) the music classes here. He
6) _____ (love) playing the guitar. In the evenings
we often 7) _____ (watch) a film together or play
computer games. It 8) _____ (be) great fun!

See you soon,

Jacob

3 Complete these questions with the verbs in brackets and *do* or *does*.

1 ___*Do*___ you ___*have*___ (have) a hobby?
2 _____ she _____ (like) music?
3 _____ they _____ (enjoy) taking photos?
4 _____ we _____ (start) our painting class today?
5 _____ Liam _____ (collect) anything?
6 _____ I _____ (buy) my ticket for the dance show here?
7 _____ your teacher _____ (sing)?

4 Match the questions (1–6) with the answers (A–F).

1 Do you go shopping with your parents? __*D*__
2 Does your sister go to a chess club? _____
3 Do Ben and Karen do painting at school? _____
4 Do they go to the cinema? _____
5 Does Matthew collect anything? _____
6 Does Jane play the piano or the guitar? _____

A Yes, she does. She goes to a club at school.
B Yes, they love films.
C Yes, he does. He's got 600 stamps.
D Yes, I do. We go every Saturday.
E No, she doesn't. She doesn't like music.
F No, they don't. They only do drawing.

Adverbs of frequency

5 Put the words in the correct place.

~~always~~   never   not often   not usually
often   sometimes

1 _____*always*_____ 100%

2 _____

3 _____

4 _____

5 _____

6 _____ 0%

6 **Put the words in the correct order to make sentences.**

1 TV / usually / in the evening / My parents / watch / .
   My parents usually watch TV in the evening.

2 go / often / in the holidays / shopping / We / .

3 in June / There / sometimes / is / a chess competition / .

4 Kiera / never / her music lessons / enjoys / .

5 read / Jasmine / usually / comics / doesn't / .

6 always / My singing lessons / fun / are / .

7 don't / They / go / on sleepovers / often / .

7 **Look at the information about Amy and Jonathan and write sentences.**

	Amy	Jonathan
play computer games	often	not usually
go on a sleepover	sometimes	never
take photographs	not often	often
sing in the bathroom	not usually	always

1 Amy / play computer games
   Amy often plays computer games.

2 Jonathan / play computer games

3 Amy / go on a sleepover

4 Jonathan / go on a sleepover

5 Amy / take photographs

6 Jonathan / take photographs

7 Amy / sing in the bathroom

8 Jonathan / sing in the bathroom

many/much

8 **Complete the table with these words.**

books   friends   fun   hobbies   money
music   people   time

much	many
	books

9 **Complete the dialogues with *much* or *many*.**

1 How _____ *many* _____ musical instruments do you play?
   Two – the piano and the violin.

2 Have you got _____ music on your MP3 player?
   Yeah, I've got about 300 songs on it.

3 How _____ people go to the chess club?
   About twelve.

4 Do you have _____ free time?
   Not after school, but I do at weekends.

5 I want a new hobby, but I don't have _____ money.
   My hobby's singing. It's free.

6 Do you like shopping?
   Yes, but there aren't _____ good shops in my town.

02 Can't live without it?

VOCABULARY

1 Complete the crossword.

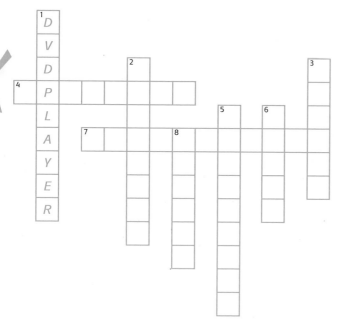

Across

4 You listen to music through these

7 A telephone you can use anywhere

Down

1 You watch DVDs on this

2 The part of a computer you use to type words

3 The part of a computer you look at to read information

5 A small gadget for listening to music

6 Something you use to move around the screen of a computer

8 A small computer that you can move easily

2 Choose the correct words.

1 Can we watch the film at your house?
Sorry, my brother's using the computer and our *MP3 player/DVD player* isn't working.

2 Don't eat your lunch at the computer! You're dropping food on the *keyboard/screen*.
OK, Dad. Sorry.

3 Rachel, your dinner's on the table. Put your *speakers/mobile phone* down, please.
OK, but can I send one quick text to Emma, please, Mum?

4 Can you play music on your laptop?
Yes, but the *keyboard/speakers* aren't very good so the music's not very loud.

5 Why are you closing the curtains?
The sun's shining on my laptop and I can't read the information on the *screen/MP3 player*.

6 How do I open this file?
Move the arrow on top of it and then click the button on the *speakers/mouse*.

3 Match the sentence beginnings (1–6) with the endings (A–F).

1 Oscar is sending _F_

2 Olivia and Sophia surf _____

3 I'm listening to music with _____

4 Every Sunday Nathan chats _____

5 It's cheap and easy to download _____

6 They're looking at _____

A my headphones.

B music.

C online with his cousins in Venezuela.

D a website about street dancing.

E the Internet together in the evenings.

F an email to his teacher about his homework.

4 Complete the sentences with these words.

> download   email   headphones   ~~online~~
> surfing   texts   webcam

1 Nicky likes chatting to her friends ___online___ .
2 Dean and Andrew _____ all their music.
3 I enjoy _____ the Internet in the evening.
4 Rebecca sends lots of _____ with her new phone.
5 I listen to music with my _____ on the bus.
6 They're sending a long _____ to their friends in France.
7 Our grandparents in Australia can see us with our new _____ .

5 Choose the best answer, A, B or C.

1 Look at this new _____ . It tells you the time and it is a torch and an MP3 player.
   (A) gadget   **B** camcorder   **C** Xbox
2 This _____ is amazing! It walks and talks.
   A watch   **B** robot   **C** laptop
3 I'm making a film of our family with my new _____ .
   A camcorder   **B** Xbox   **C** robot
4 Do you like my new _____ ? It shows what time it is in ten different countries.
   A mouse   **B** webcam   **C** watch
5 My mum's new _____ is really cool. She's reading something on it now.
   A keyboard   **B** camcorder   **C** e-book
6 Michael and Poppy love playing on their _____ . They have lots of different games.
   A Xbox   **B** robot   **C** screen

6 Complete the text with these words.

> computers   Internet   ~~laptop~~   mobile
> online   reads   send   surf

How much technology does your family use?
My brother and I have a 1) ___laptop___ each. We often 2) _____ emails and 3) _____ the Internet. My granddad's got an e-book and he 4) _____ every day. My dad doesn't like 5) _____ , but he does have a 6) _____ phone. He has to take it with him to work. My mum doesn't have a laptop, but she gets the 7) _____ on her phone. She loves shopping 8) _____ .

7 Complete the sentences with these words.

> bored   ~~diary~~   entrance   experiments
> great   hard

1 I write what I'm thinking about and feeling in my ___diary___ .
2 My new mobile phone is _____ . I love it!
3 All my friends are busy and I've got nothing to do. I feel really _____ .
4 You go into the building through the main _____ .
5 We do lots of cool _____ in our science lessons.
6 This online maths test is very _____ . I don't understand any of the questions.

8 Choose the correct words.

Hi, Bart
You aren't answering your mobile 1) *phone*/*text* and I need your help! I hope you see this 2) *note*/*email* soon. I'm doing my homework on today's science 3) *entrance*/*experiment* and I can't find my notes. Can you 4) *send*/*write* me an email with the teacher's questions? I think all the answers are 5) *mobile*/*online*. Do you remember the 6) *website*/*Internet* we need to look at?
Thanks
Tom

GRAMMAR
Present continuous

1 Complete the table with the *-ing* form of the verbs.

ride	1)	*riding*
get	2)	
have	3)	
hit	4)	
make	5)	
win	6)	
drive	7)	
sit	8)	

2 Put the words in the correct order to make sentences.

1 some robots / are / Jack and Liam / looking at / .
   Jack and Liam are looking at some robots.

2 writing / Deborah / in her school diary / is / .

3 a science experiment / are / The students / doing / .

4 watching a film / am / on my laptop / I / .

5 Oscar / a photo / is / on his mobile / taking / .

6 about King Henry VIII / We / reading / are / on the Internet / .

3 Choose the correct words.

1 The DVD player *isn't/aren't* working.
2 James *is/are* waiting for us.
3 My parents *is/are* watching a film in the lounge.
4 Helen *aren't/isn't* feeling well.
5 The children *is/are* playing computer games.
6 It *aren't/isn't* raining now.

4 Complete the sentences with the present continuous form of the verbs in brackets. Use contractions when possible.

1 We ___'re talking___ (talk) to my dad in Dubai.
2 Martin and Noah _____ (play) a computer game.
3 They _____ (download) a film from the Internet.
4 I _____ (text) my friend Suzanna.
5 Carl _____ (write) his English essay on his laptop.
6 Marie and Didier _____ (look) for a good music website.
7 You _____ (send) a lot of texts to your friend.
8 I _____ (make) a short film with my camcorder.

5 Complete the sentences about Ella's family. Use these words and use contractions when possible.

> eat / a cake   read / a book
> sleep / on the rug   talk / on the phone
> ~~watch / TV~~   work / on a laptop

1 Ella _____ *'s watching TV.*
2 Charlie _____
3 Ella's mum _____
4 Ella's dad _____
5 Ella's grandma _____
6 Ella's dog and cat _____

6 Choose the best answer, A, B or C.

1 My dad usually drives us to school, but today we
   .... the bus.
   A take   (B) are taking   C is taking

2 Mr Pritchard .... us today because our
   teacher is ill.
   A is teaching
   B teach
   C teaches

3 .... to his MP3 player at the moment?
   A Are Robbie listening
   B Does Robbie listen
   C Is Robbie listening

4 Henry .... football today. He's not
   feeling very well.
   A doesn't play
   B isn't playing
   C not playing

5 Every year we .... to a music festival
   with my cousins.
   A go   B are going   C goes

6 Look, Jack's over there. He .... his lunch
   with his friends.
   A is having   B are having   C has

7 Complete the email with the present simple or
present continuous form of the verbs in brackets.
Use contractions when possible.

Hi, Kiera
How are you? Are you having a good holiday? I
1) _'m staying_ (stay) at my grandparents' house
for the holidays. They 2) .... (live) in the
mountains. It's an amazing place. There
3) .... (be) lots of things to do here.
Every day we 4) .... (go) fishing or
horse-riding. It's great fun. I can't phone you
because there 5) .... (not be) a signal for
my mobile phone at my grandparents' house. I
6) .... (write) this email in an Internet
café in town. My grandparents 7) ....
(do) some shopping.
I hope you 8) .... (have) a good time.
See you next week!
Jennie

8 Complete the conversation with one word in each
space.

Laura

Are 1) ____you____ going
home now?

Paul

No, I'm 2) .... to my
cousin's house. I 3) ....
staying with him at the moment.

Laura

Really? Why?

Paul

My parents 4) .... doing some work
in the house. There's no electricity so the
Internet 5) .... working. I'm using
my cousin's computer for my homework.

Laura

Where 6) .... your
sister staying?

Paul

She's at my cousin's house, too. It
7) .... a really big house so
there 8) .... a bedroom for
me and my sister.

Revision Units 1 – 2

VOCABULARY

1 Choose the best answer, A, B or C.

1 I love _____. I often make cakes with my mum.
   A drawing   B singing   **C** cooking

2 Harriet has a new _____. She does her homework on it.
   A laptop   B camera   C screen

3 Every Friday, Jack goes to the _____ with his friends. He loves films.
   A sleepover   B cinema   C shopping

4 Freya loves looking at _____ about famous people.
   A webcams   B speakers   C websites

5 Charlie collects _____. He's got about 500.
   A reading   B postcards   C shopping

6 My brother's got a new _____. He reads it all the time.
   A e-book   B mobile   C camcorder

2 Complete Damien's description of his room with these words.

> comics   email   ~~laptop~~   listen   painting
> play   read   watch

> Hi. My name's Damien and this is my bedroom. My favourite thing in my room is my 1) _laptop_. I 2) _____ films, 3) _____ to music and 4) _____ my friends on it. I've also got a guitar, but I don't 5) _____ it very often. My hobby at the moment is 6) _____. On my desk I've got all my brushes and paper. At the moment I'm doing a picture of my dog, Barney. I've got lots of books and 7) _____ in my room. I always 8) _____ before I go to bed. I'm reading a great book about robots at the moment.

3 Choose the correct words.

1 Can I use your *laptop*/*headphones*, please? I want to send an email to my sister.
   Yes, of course. Here you are.

2 Where's your sister?
   She's having a *singing*/*cooking* lesson. She wants to be a pop star!

3 Do you know how to play *chess*/*the violin*?
   No, but my brother does. He loves music.

4 This website's great.
   Yeah, I know. I *download*/*surf* all my music from it.

5 What are you watching?
   It's a *film*/*TV programme* about tigers. It's on every day for half an hour.

6 I can't read my emails because the sun's shining on the computer *mouse*/*screen*.
   I can close the curtains for you.

4 Match the sentences (1–8) with the sentences (A–H).

1 Robert loves cooking.   _F_
2 My mum's got a new mobile phone.   _____
3 I always buy my clothes online.   _____
4 My sister's good at playing the guitar.   _____
5 Rachel never sends emails to her friends.   _____
6 My dad and brother are fishing together.   _____
7 My brother's not asleep.   _____
8 Georgia often goes on a sleepover.   _____

A She always sends texts.
B She plays in a rock band at school.
C They're over there on my granddad's boat.
D This is my favourite website for jeans.
E He's listening to music with his headphones.
F He often makes dinner for his family at the weekends.
G She's staying at Clare's house today.
H It's got a great camera on it.

GRAMMAR

1 Complete these questions with *much* or *many*.

1 How _*much*_ time do you spend on your computer?
2 How _____ texts do you send every day?
3 How _____ music do you download every month?
4 How _____ DVDs do you have?
5 How _____ shopping do you do online?
6 How _____ computer games do you own?
7 How _____ people in your class have a laptop?
8 How _____ does this computer game cost?

2 Complete the conversation with the present simple or present continuous form of the verbs in brackets. Use contractions where possible.

Emilia

Hi, Isaac. What (1) _are you doing_ (you/do)?

Isaac

Hi, Emilia. I (2) _____ (paint) a picture of my mum.

Emilia

Is it for school?

Isaac

No, it's for the art club. I (3) _____ (go) every Wednesday.

Emilia

Oh, right. (4) _____ (be) it good fun?

Isaac

Yes, I (5) _____ (love) it. We (6) _____ (learn) to paint faces at the moment.

Emilia

(7) _____ (you/draw) as well?

Isaac

Yes, we (8) _____ (do) different kinds of art every week.

Emilia

Great! Can I join?

3 Put the words in the correct order to make sentences.

1 always / I / from / download / this website / my music / .
   I always download my music from this website.
2 after school / watch / We / usually / DVDs / don't / .
   _____
3 with / sometimes / Oliver / photos / his mobile / takes / .
   _____
4 never / computer games / They / at school / play / .
   _____
5 chat / Sophie and Alex / don't / online / often / .
   _____
6 in the evenings / usually / on his laptop / works / My dad / .
   _____

4 Complete the advert with these words.

are   have   is   ~~looking~~   make   starting

Sanders Street Leisure Centre

New Computer Club!

Are you 1) _looking_ for a new hobby and 2) _____ you between 13 and 16 years old? Then we have the answer for you!

The leisure centre is 3) _____ a new computer club. It's on Thursday afternoons from 4 to 5.30 p.m.

At the club you can play computer games and also 4) _____ your own games. We 5) _____ more information online on our website. The club 6) _____ free but there are only 20 places.

We hope to see you soon!

We ♥ school

VOCABULARY

1 Find and write eight school subjects.

k	g	e	c	u	g	e	l	i	h	b	m	d	s	s
i	h	t	s	m	b	t	k	f	s	o	t	m	e	r
m	e	s	r	u	n	y	o	i	n	c	e	i	l	i
l	n	h	i	s	t	o	r	y	e	k	d	o	n	e
o	i	o	p	i	n	c	e	n	t	u	i	n	o	d
p	m	u	o	c	i	s	o	b	t	s	o	p	s	y
o	a	c	n	u	k	i	w	s	o	c	u	n	m	p
l	a	r	t	j	i	c	r	o	c	i	k	n	a	d
l	s	b	u	a	s	e	n	t	o	e	n	u	t	r
i	w	a	x	b	t	u	o	n	i	n	n	c	h	e
t	o	n	i	u	c	o	m	p	u	c	a	t	s	o
i	n	o	p	e	d	i	a	s	n	e	a	p	s	d
g	o	m	a	t	s	y	u	d	i	o	m	u	i	o
i	o	n	w	g	e	o	g	r	a	p	h	y	s	a
c	r	a	n	k	i	o	n	i	c	a	w	h	o	c

1	_art_	**2**	
3		**4**	
5		**6**	
7		**8**	

2 Match these places with the objects.

> ~~canteen~~   classroom   gym   library
> science lab   sports field

1 _canteen_   **2** _____

3 _____   **4** _____

5 _____   **6** _____

3 Complete the dialogues with these words.

> canteen   classroom   ~~gym~~   library
> science lab   sports field

1 Why have you got your sports bag, Alex?
I've got basketball practice in the _gym_
after school.
2 Are you having lunch in the _____, Lucy?
No, I'm going home for lunch today.
3 Where are we having geography today?
_____ 12B. It's next to the gym.
4 Where are you going, Isobel?
To the _____ . I've got chemistry now.
5 What are all those books for?
For my history project. I'm taking them back to
the _____ .
6 What's happening on the _____ ?
They're having a football match.

4 Complete the table with these words and phrases.

> an exam   a good mark   a language
> a prize   a school uniform   a test   a tie
> French   in your notebook   on the board

get	
have/do	*an exam*
learn	
wear	
write	

5 Choose the correct words.

1 I *had/wrote* a lot of history homework last night.
2 Most students in my country *do/wear* a uniform to school.
3 Emily *did/got* a good mark in her chemistry test.
4 The teacher *wrote/wore* the answers on the board.
5 I *wear/get* a red tie to school every day.
6 Every July we *write/have* exams.

6 Match the words (1–8) with the definitions (A–H).

1 board *E*
2 desk ___
3 exam ___
4 mark ___
5 notebook ___
6 pencil case ___
7 timetable ___
8 school uniform ___

A a list of times when classes start and finish
B a number or letter that shows how good a piece of work is
C a small bag where you keep your pens and pencils
D a special set of clothes that students wear for school
E something on the wall of a classroom that the teacher writes on
F a test of how much you know about something
G a book you can write in
H a table that you sit at to write or work

7 Choose the correct words.

1 The *music/art* teacher wasn't at school so we didn't have guitar practice today.
2 Your *timetable/board* shows you when lessons start and finish.
3 Henry got a good mark for his English language *prize/test*.
4 I can't go to the cinema. I've got a lot of *homework/exam* to do.
5 My school *tie/uniform* is a green sweater and a black skirt.
6 Jaya sits at the *desk/classroom* behind James.

8 Complete the text with the best answer, A, B or C, for each space.

MY SCHOOL

I like going to school because I see my best friends there. All the students wear a 1) _____ at my school. It's blue and it looks OK, but I don't like wearing a 2) _____ . It's so uncomfortable round my neck!

We don't sit in the same 3) _____ all day. We move for each lesson. I never remember what lesson I have so I'm always looking at my 4) _____ !

My favourite 5) _____ is French. Our French teacher is really cool. We never sit at our desks all lesson. We often get up and write on the 6) _____ . We had a French exam last week. I was really happy with my 7) _____ because I got 19/20.

I don't like history very much. Our history teacher always gives us lots of 8) _____ !

	A		B		C	
1	(A) uniform		B bag		C glasses	
2	A skirt		B trousers		C tie	
3	A table		B classroom		C teacher	
4	A watch		B pencil case		C timetable	
5	A subject		B classroom		C desk	
6	A board		B desk		C pen	
7	A classroom		B timetable		C mark	
8	A games		B homework		C prizes	

GRAMMAR

1 Complete the table with the correct form of the verbs.

Infinitive	Past simple
write	1) _____ *wrote*
2) _____	went
take	3) _____
4) _____	saw
choose	5) _____
6) _____	was/were
speak	7) _____
8) _____	began

2 Complete the sentences with *was/were* or *wasn't/weren't*.

1 It _____ *was* _____ Jonathan's first day at school today. He really enjoyed it.
2 I usually enjoy my lunch in the canteen, but today the food _____ very nice.
3 I don't usually like maths, but my lesson _____ really good today.
4 Jacob and Emily _____ at school today. They aren't very well.
5 My English homework _____ very difficult today. I finished it quickly.
6 I got a really good mark in my history exam. My parents _____ really happy.

3 Complete the short answers.

1 Were George and Harry in class today?
Yes, _____ *they were* _____ .
2 Was your homework difficult?
No, _____ .
3 Were your friends in the canteen at lunchtime?
Yes, _____ .
4 Was your school uniform red and grey?
Yes, _____ .
5 Were you nervous before your exam today, Joe?
No, _____ .
6 Was Anna the winner of the art prize this year?
Yes, _____ .

4 Complete the sentences with the past simple form of the verbs in brackets.

1 Our teacher _____ *wrote* _____ (write) the questions on the board.
2 I _____ (choose) Italian for my foreign language subject.
3 Mr Carter _____ (not give) us any geography homework yesterday.
4 Lee _____ (speak) to the PE teacher about the basketball match.
5 I _____ (have) lunch with Grace in the canteen.
6 The students _____ (not wear) school uniform yesterday.
7 We _____ (begin) the exam at 9.45 a.m.

5 Complete the text with the correct form of the verbs in brackets.

My year in Greece

When I was 13 we 1) _____lived_____ (live) in Greece for a year. My school in Greece was called 'Gymnasio'. My school day 2) _____ (not be) the same as in the UK. In my Greek school, lessons 3) _____ (begin) at 8.15 and 4) _____ (finish) at 1.45.

The school 5) _____ (not have) a canteen. Everyone 6) _____ (go) home for lunch. We usually 7) _____ (have) lunch at about 2.30.

I loved the school summer holidays in Greece. They 8) _____ (be) three months long!

Past simple questions

6 Put the words in the correct order to make questions.

1 today / your maths exam / Was / difficult / ?
   Was your maths exam difficult today?

2 finish / you / your history homework / Did / ?
   _____

3 a good mark / Did / get / in his biology test / David / ?
   _____

4 the answer on the board / the teacher / Did / write / ?
   _____

5 your library books / Were / in your school bag / ?
   _____

6 Clare and Mark / lunch in the school canteen / Did / have / ?
   _____

7 Match the questions (1–6) with the answers (A–F).

1 Did Madeleine have a good English lesson? _B_
2 How much was it? _____
3 Did you get a good mark for your exam? _____
4 Where was your PE lesson today? _____
5 Did Jake and Sonia have school dinner today? _____
6 When did you leave school yesterday? _____

A At 3.15 p.m.
B Yes, she did.
C No, they didn't.
D £2.99.
E Yes, I did.
F In the gym.

8 Complete the email with these words.

did   didn't   had   saw   took   ~~was~~
was   went

Hi, Billy

How 1) _____was_____ your school trip?
2) _____ you have a good time? I came back from my school history trip yesterday.

We 3) _____ to London. We 4) _____ a really good time. We visited lots of old places. My favourite place 5) _____ the Tower of London. We also went to Buckingham Palace, but we 6) _____ see the Queen! I 7) _____ lots of photos for my school project. We also went to the cinema in Leicester Square one evening. We 8)_____ a really good film.

Speak soon,

Helen

VOCABULARY

1 Put the letters in the right order to make different types of shops.

1 lhcoste ohps — _clothes shop_
2 kuspemaretr — ....
3 ucsim hosp — ....
4 osokhobp — ....
5 tsorps hops — ....
6 pocmrute hsop — ....

2 Choose the correct words.

1 What's the *price/receipt* of this bag?
2 We have a great *card/market* in our town. It sells everything and is really cheap.
3 My mum bought the concert tickets online with her *card/cash*.
4 Have you got the *price/receipt* for my slippers, Mum? I want to return them to the shop.
5 Have you got any *cash/receipt*? They don't take cards in this shop.

3 Match the meanings (1–6) with the words (A–F).

1 the opposite of *open* _C_
2 a person who buys something from a shop ....
3 someone who sells things in a shop ....
4 a large shop that sells many types of things ....
5 to put on clothes in a shop before you buy them ....
6 something that is less than its usual price ....

A customer
B shop assistant
C closed
D bargain
E try on
F department store

4 Match these words with the pictures.

~~card~~   cash   market   price   receipt

1 _card_

2 ....

3 ....

4 ....

5 ....

5 Complete the conversation with these words.

> bargain   closed   customer
> ~~department store~~   open
> shop assistant   try on

Lara

Hi, Emma. Did you know there's a new
1) _department store_ in town?

Emma

Yeah, I know, Hartley's. My cousin's a
2) _____ there.

Lara

Really? I went there at the weekend with my
mum. I saw some great clothes. I want to
3) _____ some jeans I saw.

Emma

OK, great. My cousin said there are some
half-price trainers, they're a real
4) _____ ! I want to
get some with my birthday money. What
time do you want to go?

Lara

Well, it's 5) _____ every
day. It's only 6) _____ on
Sunday afternoons.

Emma

Great. Let's go tomorrow, then. And I think for the
first month every new 7) _____
gets a free magazine.

Lara

Cool!

6 Match the sentence beginnings (1–6) with the endings (a–f).

1 I'm saving
2 My dad paid
3 It cost
4 I bought
5 Thomas sold
6 We spent

a us nothing. It was free.
b a new dress for my party.
c his bike to a friend.
d the bill in the restaurant.
e money for a holiday.
f a lot of money on computer games.

7 Choose the correct words.

1 My new jeans were a bargain. They only *paid*/*cost* £15.
2 Fiona's *saving*/*collecting* her birthday money because she wants to buy a guitar.
3 They *bought*/*paid* a new computer game at the weekend.
4 Noah doesn't *buy*/*spend* a lot of money on music.
5 My grandma *paid*/*bought* for my tennis lessons.
6 How much does this bracelet *buy*/*cost*?

8 Match the questions (1–6) with the answers (A–F).

1 How much are these jeans? _D_
2 Where are the customer toilets? _____
3 Have you got your receipt? _____
4 Can I pay by card? _____
5 How much is this book? _____
6 Where's the shop assistant? _____

A Next to the men's clothing department.
B Sorry, we only take cash.
C The price is on the back of it.
D They're £59.99.
E Over there. She's wearing a red uniform.
F Yes, it's in my bag.

GRAMMAR
Comparative and superlative adjectives

1 Complete the table with the comparative form of these adjectives.

> ~~bad~~ big busy difficult expensive good pretty short

-er	-ier	more + adjective	irregular
			worse

2 Choose the correct words.

1 The jacket is _more expensive_/_expensiver_ than the trousers.
2 The green bag is _nicer_/_more nice_ than the red one.
3 The shop assistants are _helpfuller_/_more helpful_ here than in the other shop.
4 Online shopping is _more easy_/_easier_ than going to the shops.
5 The sports clothes in the market are _cheaper_/_more cheaper_ than the ones here.
6 The prices are _better_/_more good_ here than in the other shop.

3 Complete the sentences with the comparative form of the adjectives in brackets.

1 Your jacket is _____newer_____ (new) than mine.
2 This book is _____ (interesting) than that one.
3 I think shopping is _____ (boring) than doing homework.
4 Their shopping bags are _____ (heavy) than ours.
5 This birthday card is _____ (funny) than the other one.
6 The music in this shop is _____ (bad) than in the last shop.
7 I think the red dress is _____ (beautiful) than the blue one.
8 This music shop is _____ (big) than the one in my town.

4 Complete the table.

Adjective	Superlative
popular	1) _____most popular_____
2) _____	worst
big	3) _____
4) _____	farthest/furthest
difficult	5) _____
6) _____	lightest
good	7) _____
8) _____	friendliest

5 Complete the sentences with the superlative form of these words.

> ~~expensive~~ heavy old small tasty young

1 This is the ___most expensive___ phone in the shop.

2 These are Joshua's _____ pair of jeans.

3 My rucksack is the _____ .

4 Sally is the _____ shop assistant.

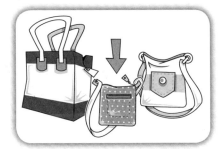

5 I like the _____ bag.

6 This is the _____ cake.

6 Complete the sentences with one word in each space.

1 This is ___*the*___ best sports shop in town.
2 Shopping online is often cheaper _____ buying things at the shops.
3 Your trainers are _____ expensive than mine.
4 The department store is busier at the weekend _____ in the week.
5 It's always _____ fun shopping with friends than with your parents.
6 This is _____ worst clothes shop in my town.

7 Choose the correct words.

1 The clothes are *cheaper*/*cheapest* here than in the last shop.
2 I've got the *most heaviest*/*heaviest* shopping bags.
3 Frank is *younger*/*youngest* than Lilly.
4 Our bill was *bigger*/*biggest* than yours.
5 The market was *busiest*/*busier* than the supermarket.
6 There are lots of clothes shops in my town, but Hardy's is the *most*/*more* popular.

8 Complete the review with the best answer, A, B or C for each space.

Some people say New York is a great city for shopping. What do I think? – Yes! I went shopping in New York last weekend and had the 1) _____ shopping experience. Why? There are lots of reasons. Firstly, the shops are 2) _____ than the shops in my city and there is so much choice. Secondly, the shop assistants are 3) _____ than in many other places. You can also find 4) _____ bargains in New York! I bought some jeans and they were $30 5) _____ than the normal price. There are also lots of 6) _____ places to stop and have lunch. My favourite is Papa Joe's Pizzeria. They make the 7) _____ pizzas!

1 **A** amazing
 B most amazing
 C more amazing
2 **A** big
 B biggest
 C bigger
3 **A** friendlier
 B friendliest
 C friendly
4 **A** greatest
 B great
 C greater than
5 **A** cheap
 B cheapest
 C cheaper
6 **A** cool
 B cooler
 C coolest
7 **A** good
 B better
 C best

Revision Units 3 – 4

VOCABULARY

1 Match these words with the correct meaning.

> canteen ~~cash~~ classroom gym
> library market price receipt

1 This is money in coins or notes.
   cash

2 This is a place you do exercise.

3 You get this piece of paper when you buy something.

4 This is where you eat lunch at school.

5 This is how much something costs.

6 There are lots of books in this place.

7 There are desks and a board in this place.

8 People buy and sell things in this place.

2 Choose the correct verbs.

1 Hannah *did/got* a prize for her painting.
2 Mark and Andrew *have/wear* a blue uniform to school.
3 We *had/wrote* a geography exam last Monday.
4 My parents *paid/bought* my new bike for me.
5 We didn't *learn/have* French lessons at primary school.
6 Tom *spent/saved* all his birthday money on a new guitar.

3 Choose the correct words.

1 Why didn't you buy the skirt you liked?
   Because the shop was *closed/open* when I arrived.
2 Do you like these jeans? I bought them yesterday.
   Yes, they're great. How much did they *pay/cost*?
3 I bought this jacket yesterday, but it's the wrong size. Can I change it?
   Yes, of course. Have you got your *receipt/bargain*?
4 Excuse me, have you got a smaller jacket?
   Yes, here you are. Would you like to *try/have* it on?
5 I like this bag. How much is it?
   Oh, it's a real *price/bargain*. It's only £12.
6 Who *paid/spent* for your football lessons?
   I did. I saved all my birthday money.

4 Complete Charlotte's diary with these words.

> assistant case field homework
> lesson shopping ~~teacher~~ test

Tuesday 8 June

Today didn't start very well! I got to school late and my 1) _____teacher_____ wasn't very happy with me. My first 2) _____ was maths. We had a 3) _____ – it was really difficult! French was OK, but Mrs Chevalier gave us lots of 4) _____ to do! In the afternoon I had PE and we played hockey on the sports 5) _____. It was a great game and our team won. After school I went 6) _____ with Mum. She bought me a new pencil 7) _____ and some cool trainers. The shop 8) _____ gave me a free drinks bottle with my trainers. Then Mum took me for a burger and chips. We saw the new boy from school with his dad.

GRAMMAR

1 Complete these sentences with the comparative or superlative form of the adjectives in brackets.

1 Riverside is _the largest_ (large) secondary school in the city.

2 Yasmin got a _____ (high) mark in her test than Annabel.

3 I think Mr Unwin is _____ (funny) teacher at school.

4 History is _____ (difficult) subject at school.

5 Your school uniform is _____ (bad) than mine.

6 Gareth got a prize for _____ (good) science project.

7 Sally's got _____ (neat) handwriting in the class.

8 Our new library is _____ (big) than our old one.

2 Complete Amy's email with the past simple form of these verbs.

be   buy   go   have   see   spend
stop   take

Hi Harriet

How are you? I 1) _went_ shopping in London with my parents yesterday. There 2) _____ lots of fantastic clothes shops. I 3) _____ two new tops and a pair of jeans. We 4) _____ at a café in Covent Garden for lunch. I 5) _____ a really cool girl there. She 6) _____ purple hair and a white leather dress! In the afternoon we 7) _____ my little brother to Hamley's. It's the world's largest toyshop. We 8) _____ lots of money there!

See you at school tomorrow.

Love Amy x

3 Complete the short answers.

1 Did Mark buy an expensive jacket?
Yes, _he did_ .

2 Were Jamie and Zoe in school today?
No, _____ .

3 Was your homework easy?
No, _____ .

4 Did you like your school lunch?
Yes, _____ .

5 Was this your best mark for English?
Yes, _____ .

6 Did your sister go on the school trip with you?
No, _____ .

4 Choose the best answer, A, B or C.

1 The shoes are more expensive here _____ in the other shop.
   A with   **B** from   **C** than

2 Freddie _____ his school tie in the gym yesterday.
   A leave   **B** left   **C** leaves

3 What mark did Annalise _____ in her English exam last week?
   A got   **B** get   **C** gets

4 Is this _____ cheapest bookshop in town?
   A the   **B** a   **C** one

5 Rachel is _____ than Tom at maths.
   A good   **B** better   **C** best

6 Ms Pinner _____ teach me science last year.
   A didn't   **B** doesn't   **C** don't

05 Mysteries from history

VOCABULARY

1 Match these words with the meanings.

> ancient   battle   castle   famous
> king   ~~queen~~   treasure

1 a female head of a country
   queen

2 a large strong building with high walls

3 from a long time ago

4 a male head of a country

5 something or someone that many people know

6 a fight between two armies in a war

7 valuable objects such as gold, silver and jewellery

2 Complete the sentences with these words.

> ancient   battle   castle   famous
> ~~king~~   queen   treasure

1 Tutankhamun was a _____*king*_____ in Egypt.
2 The _____ Greeks held the first Olympic Games.
3 Prince Charles's mother is _____ Elizabeth II.
4 Lots of people know about the Colosseum in Rome. It's very _____ .
5 The _____ of Little Bighorn in 1876 was between the US army and the Native Americans.
6 The pirates found _____ on the ship. It was a big box of gold jewellery.
7 No kings or queens live in Chapultepec _____ in Mexico. It is a museum.

3 Complete the table with these words and phrases.

> ~~2.30 p.m.~~   25 May 1975   April 2008
> the twenty-first century   2 January 1952
> the beginning of last year
> 12 o'clock   the thirteenth century

at	*2.30 p.m.*
in	
on	

4 Choose the best answer, A, B or C.

1 It's my brother's birthday _____ Friday.
   (A) on   **B** at   **C** in
2 The battle finished on _____ .
   A 26 June 1876
   B June 1876
   C 1876
3 The museum opened _____ the end of last year.
   A in   **B** at   **C** on
4 Queen Isabella I of Castile was born _____ 22 April 1451.
   A on   **B** at   **C** in
5 They found the treasure of Gourdon in France in the middle _____ the nineteenth century.
   A to   **B** on   **C** of
6 Kings of England lived in the castle many years _____ .
   A from   **B** ago   **C** for

5 Find and write six adjectives.

g	o	u	g	l	d	l	e	s	k
o	n	t	e	o	a	h	n	r	y
n	t	i	n	f	n	o	a	f	e
c	o	h	d	s	g	d	e	n	t
l	i	g	h	t	e	m	a	n	d
e	l	l	e	a	r	o	u	c	e
e	n	o	l	l	o	g	i	l	t
n	o	n	u	s	u	n	t	e	r
k	r	a	a	d	s	c	e	a	n
s	o	d	i	r	t	y	i	n	n

1 _____*loud*_____
2 _____
3 _____
4 _____
5 _____
6 _____

6 Choose the correct words.

1 It's not a good idea to walk here at night. It's very *safe/dangerous*.
2 This city is very *dirty/clean*. There's rubbish everywhere.
3 Before electricity, homes were often very *light/dark*.
4 Life was very hard for *poor/rich* people in Victorian England.
5 The sound of the battle was very *loud/quiet*. You could hear it for miles.
6 In history it was always *rich/quiet* people who lived in castles.

7 Choose the odd one out.

1 the 1980s
  1200 BC
  December
  the sixteenth century
2 castle
  treasure
  palace
  museum
3 battle
  famous
  quiet
  ancient
4 12 o'clock
  2001
  in the morning
  4.55 p.m.
5 queen
  tower
  prince
  king
6 dangerous
  history
  poor
  dirty

8 Complete the text with these words.

> 1901   dangerous   dark   ~~in~~   poor
>   queen   rich

What was life like in Victorian times?

The Victorian times started 1) _____*in*_____
1837 and ended in 2) _____. This is
when Victoria was 3) _____ of Britain.
The people who lived in Britain at this time
were called Victorians. Many 4) _____
Victorians had an easy and comfortable life, but
5) _____ Victorians had a very hard life.
Many poor people lived in 6) _____ ,
dirty houses. Their jobs were sometimes
7) _____ and they worked long hours.

GRAMMAR
Past continuous

1 **Choose the correct words.**

1 The king *eat/was eating* dinner.
2 Mark and Jane *was/were* visiting a castle.
3 He *watch/was watching* a film about the Romans.
4 We *was/were* looking at a website about the pyramids.
5 Martin *search/was searching* for treasure.
6 I *was/were* listening to a radio programme about the Incas.

2 **Make sentences. Use the past continuous.**

1 the soldiers / fight / in the battle
   The soldiers were fighting in the battle.
2 the children / hide / the treasure / ?

3 the king and queen / not stay / in the castle

4 we / study / ancient Greece

5 Henry / not speak / to his brother

6 she / visit / the Natural History Museum / ?

3 **Complete the short answers.**

1 Were you visiting the museum when you saw Mark?
   Yes, _____ *I was* _____.
2 Were they studying the Romans in their history lesson on Monday?
   Yes, _____.
3 Was he searching for treasure when he found the cave?
   No, _____.
4 Were you waiting for a long time, Alice?
   No, _____.
5 Were the Aztecs in Mexico in the fourteenth to sixteenth centuries?
   Yes, _____.
6 Were your parents watching a film when you got home?
   No, _____.

4 **Complete the sentences with the past simple or past continuous form of the verbs in brackets.**

1 She _was watching_ (watch) the news when she _____heard_____ (hear) the loud noise outside.
2 Kieran and Joe _____ (find) the old watch when they _____ (dig) in the school garden.
3 I _____ (stand) outside the palace when I _____ (see) the queen.
4 We _____ (work) on the computer when the room suddenly _____ (go) dark.
5 The tour guide _____ (tell) us about the castle when my phone _____ (ring).
6 The man _____ (drive) home when the police _____ (stop) him.
7 They _____ (have) dinner when they _____ (hear) the news.
8 Laura _____ (watch) a film when she _____ (fall) asleep.

5 **Complete the text with the best answer, A, B or C, for each space.**

Treasure!

It was the end of the summer and my brother and I 1)_____ spending our last day at the beach. It was a hot day and the sun was shining so we 2)_____ to go for a swim. We 3)_____ in the sea when we noticed a dark hole in the rocks. We swam closer and realised it was a cave. We 4)_____ feeling a bit scared, but decided to swim inside. When we got inside we 5)_____ something bright at the back of the cave. It 6)_____ shining and looked like silver. 'Treasure!' we both 7)_____. When we reached it, we both laughed. It 8)_____ treasure, it was some old tin cans!

	A	B	C
1	was	**(B)** were	is
2	decided	deciding	decide
3	swim	swam	were swimming
4	was	were	is
5	seeing	see	saw
6	is	was	were
7	shouted	shouting	shout
8	weren't	isn't	wasn't

Defining relative clauses

6 **Put the words in the correct order to make sentences.**

1 who / These are / lived in Windsor Castle / the kings / .

   These are the kings who lived in Windsor Castle.

2 who / Harry is / found the treasure / the boy / .

....

3 went to London / are / who / the students / Where / ?

....

4 about dinosaurs / a book / is / I'm reading / which / .

....

5 is / which / They've got / 300 years old / a painting / .

....

6 works / That's the man / in the museum / who / .

....

7 was on my desk / the map / Where's / that / ?

....

8 has information / that / This is the website / about Henry VIII / .

....

....

7 **Choose the correct words.**

1 A castle is a building *that*/*who* often has towers.
2 I met somebody *which*/*who* lives near the Acropolis in Athens.
3 Anna works in a shop *which*/*who* sells lots of old things.
4 The letter *that*/*who* is on the table is about my history trip.
5 We live in the house *that*/*who* my grandfather built.
6 We had a history test *that*/*who* was very difficult.

8 **Complete the text with these words.**

> making   standing   talking   that
> ~~was~~   was   who   who

One day last week I 1) _____*was*_____ walking home from school. I was on the road 2) _____ goes past the old castle. I was 3) _____ on my mobile phone to my friend 4) _____ was telling me a joke. I 5) _____ laughing a lot when someone said to me 'Sshh! Can you be quiet, please?' When I turned around I saw a man in old clothes. He was 6) _____ at one of the open windows in the castle. He looked angry. I switched off my phone. When I looked at the castle again, the man wasn't there. Where was the man 7) _____ spoke to me? I knew the castle wasn't someone's home. I was a bit scared. The next day I heard in the news that a TV company was 8) _____ a film in the castle. The man who was wearing old clothes was an actor!

06 Have a good trip!

VOCABULARY

1 Complete the table with these words.

~~bike~~ coach ferry helicopter
motorbike plane ship train tram yacht

Land	Air	Sea
bike		

2 Choose the correct words.

1 Are you taking your *bike/motorbike* on holiday with you?
   Yes, we're going to go cycling in the mountains.

2 Do you walk to school?
   No, I take the school *bus/yacht*.

3 Is your brother on a school trip?
   Yes. He's in Switzerland. They're on a *coach/ferry* trip through the mountains.

4 How do you travel between the islands?
   There's a small *ship/ferry*. It carries about thirty passengers.

5 What did you do for your birthday?
   My uncle took me on a *helicopter/motorbike* ride. It was my first time flying.

6 How long does it take you to travel to Moscow?
   About five hours. We usually go by *tram/train*.

7 Cannes is a very popular place for the rich and famous.
   Yes, you can see some amazing *helicopters/yachts* in the harbour.

8 What's the best way to get to the central library?
   Take the *tram/coach* because the traffic is always bad in the city centre.

3 Complete the text with these words.

catch drive ferry go helicopter
journey on foot ~~trams~~

Hi. My name's Pedro and I live on an island. The island's not big and there are no buses or 1) _____trams_____ so I usually go everywhere 2) _____. My parents both 3) _____, but they sold their car when we moved to the island. Every month we 4) _____ to the city on the mainland. First we take the 5) _____ from the harbour, and then we 6) _____ the train to the city centre. I really enjoy the 7) _____ . There is a rich businessman who lives on my island. I know he has a 8) _____ and flies to the mainland. I think that's a really cool way to travel!

4 Match these places with the pictures.

airport ~~bus stop~~ coach station
harbour port train station

1 _____bus stop_____

2 _____

3 _____

4 _____

5 _____   6 _____

5 Match the words in bold with the meanings.

1 Can all **passengers** travelling to Gloucester please get off the train now? *B*
2 How much is a train **ticket** to Istanbul? _____
3 The school is organising a weekend **trip** to Madrid. _____
4 The bus **driver** will tell you which bus stop you need. _____
5 We apologise for the **delay** to the 10.45 train to London. This train will now leave at 11.30. _____
6 Please do not leave any **luggage** in front of the train doors. _____

A someone who drives a vehicle
B a person who is using a kind of transport but is not driving it, flying it or sailing it
C when you go somewhere, usually for a short time, and come back again
D when something happens later than you planned or expected
E the bags and suitcases that you take with you when you are travelling
F a small piece of paper or card to show you paid for a journey

6 Choose the correct words.

1 How much *tickets/luggage* are you taking? I've only got one suitcase.
2 We are coming back from our skiing *trip/delay* late on Sunday evening.
3 The train didn't leave on time because the *driver/passenger* was having a tea break.
4 You need to buy a *harbour/ticket* before you get on the ferry.
5 I'll meet you at the *bus stop/bus station* near my house. It's the one in front of the post box.
6 These seats are for *tickets/passengers* who are old or disabled.

7 Complete the sentences with these words.

drives   drove   fly   ~~ride~~   rides   sailed

1 When I was seven I learned to _____*ride*_____ a horse.
2 The fisherman _____ out to sea in his fishing boat.
3 My uncle worked in London last year. He _____ a black taxi.
4 One day I'd like to learn to _____ a helicopter.
5 My brother is 18 and he _____ a motorbike.
6 My mum's a bus driver. She _____ the school bus.

8 Choose the correct words.

Hi, Jane

I'm so excited! We're going to visit my cousins in Australia next week. We're going to 1) *drive/take* a coach to Heathrow Airport. Then we're 2) *catching/flying* a plane to Singapore. We'll stay there for a few days and then 3) *ride/take* another plane to Australia. We're arriving in Sydney late at night. My uncle's meeting us at the 4) *airport/station* and he'll 5) *catch/drive* us to his house in Newcastle. My uncle's got a boat and he says he'll teach me to 6) *ride/sail*! I'll call you when I'm back.

Adam

GRAMMAR
going to

1 Make questions. Use *going to*.

1 you / travel / to Morocco / by plane / ?

Are you going to travel to Morocco by plane?

2 we / stay / for seven nights / ?

3 she / stay / with a family in Brazil / ?

4 what / you / do / next summer / ?

5 when / she / learn to drive / ?

6 Jacob / cycle / to school tomorrow / ?

7 they / meet / at the coach station / ?

2 Match the answers with the questions in exercise 1.

a I'm going to stay with my grandparents. __4__

b No, she isn't. _____

c No, they're going to meet at the train station. _____

d When she's twenty. _____

e Yes, he is. _____

f Yes, I am. _____

g Yes, we are. _____

3 Complete Harriet's plans for the weekend. Use *going to* and the verbs in brackets.

My friend Francesca 1) ___'s going to spend___ (spend) this weekend with me. I 2) _____ (meet) her on Saturday morning at the train station and we 3) _____ (walk) to the shopping centre. She wants to buy a new coat, but I 4) _____ (not buy) anything. In the evening we 5) _____ (see) some other friends and watch a DVD together. Francesca 6) _____ (stay) the night at my house. On Sunday we 7) _____ (not do) anything – just relax!

will

4 Complete the sentences with these verbs. Use *will* or *won't*.

be   buy   ~~catch~~   leave   take   walk

1 Tom's mum usually drives him home from school, but today he ___will catch___ the bus.

2 We _____ to the party because it's raining.

3 Next year my uncle _____ us to the South of France. He's very rich and has a yacht.

4 Kirsty _____ late for dinner because she missed her bus.

5 Liam's parents _____ him a motorbike. They think motorbikes are dangerous.

6 The ferry _____ on time because of the bad weather.

5 Complete the questions with *will* and these verbs. Complete the short answers with *will* or *won't*.

> buy   have   miss   ~~phone~~   send   take

1 _____Will_____ you _____phone_____ me tomorrow evening from your hotel room?
Yes, I _____will_____ .

2 _____ she _____ a lot of luggage with her when she comes?
No, she _____ .

3 _____ they _____ their friends and family?
Yes, they _____ .

4 _____ we _____ our tickets before we go?
No, we _____ .

5 _____ he _____ lots of photos to show us?
Yes, he _____ .

6 _____ you _____ me an email?
Yes, I _____ .

Present continuous for future

6 Complete the sentences. Use the present continuous form of the verbs in brackets.

1 Here are your tickets. The ferry _____'s leaving_____ (leave) in ten minutes.

2 Rachel _____ (not come) on the trip tomorrow. She's not very well.

3 Here's a picture of our new car. Mum _____ (collect) it from the garage next week.

4 I can't come with you to the café. I _____ (meet) my cousins at the train station in five minutes.

5 My brother _____ (go) to a motorbike show on Saturday. He got tickets for his birthday.

6 Simon _____ (not see) Will and Suzie this evening. He's got too much homework to do.

7 Complete the information sheet with one word in each space.

Class 9B school trip to Paris

This year our class 1) _____is_____ going to visit Paris for our school trip. We 2) _____ going to stay in Paris for two nights. We're travelling 3) _____ the port of Dover 4) _____ coach and catching a ferry to France. Then we 5) _____ travelling by coach to Paris. We're 6) _____ to stay in a hotel in the centre of the city. The trip 7) _____ cost £159 per student.

Revision Units 5 – 6

VOCABULARY

1 Match the conversations with these places.

> airport   bus-stop   castle   harbour
> museum   port

1 Excuse me, does the number 46 stop here?
No, it stops further up the road, near that big tree.
bus stop

2 So how old is this part?
It's about three hundred years old. This was the king's bedroom.
_____

3 Is this where your uncle keeps his fishing boat?
Yes, it's called Boscastle. It's only a small place. There aren't many boats here.
_____

4 What time does our plane leave?
In about half an hour. Let's look around the shops while we're waiting.
_____

5 It's really nice here. Is it very new?
Yes, it's about five years old. It's got a huge collection of ancient treasure.
_____

6 There are so many ships!
Yes, I know. It's always busy here. I love watching the big ships arrive.
_____

2 Complete the sentences with *in*, *at* or *on*.

1 Our train is leaving ___*at*___ 10.29 a.m.
2 Mary Stuart was Queen of Scotland _____ the sixteenth century.
3 We'll arrive at the airport _____ two o'clock.
4 The ship called the Mary Rose sank _____ 19 July 1545.
5 I went on a yacht for the first time _____ the weekend.
6 Tom and his family are going to Mexico _____ September.
7 We moved to a house near the harbour _____ the end of last year.
8 They're catching a coach to Cardiff _____ the morning.

3 Complete the text with these words.

> caught   delay   driver   passengers
> station   tickets   train   trip

Last month I went on a day 1) ___*trip*___ to Manchester with my parents. We bought our train 2) _____ in Birmingham and 3) _____ a train at nine o'clock. Everything was going well and then suddenly the train stopped. After a short time the 4) _____ spoke to the 5) _____ . 'I'm afraid there is a problem with the train. I'm very sorry about the 6) _____ .' At first we didn't mind. My parents were reading their newspapers and I was listening to my MP3 player. After one hour we started to get bored. Then after two hours we really wanted to get off the 7) _____ ! At 1 o'clock we finally arrived at Manchester train 8) _____ . We didn't have a lot of time to see Manchester, but the train company gave us a free ticket because of the delay so we're going back next Saturday!

4 Choose the best answer, A, B or C.

1 It is very _____ inside the castle because there aren't many windows.
   A dark   **B** loud   **C** light
2 The *Titanic* is a very _____ ship.
   A famous   **B** ancient   **C** quiet
3 This bus isn't very _____ . There's rubbish on the floor.
   A dirty   **B** clean   **C** dangerous
4 They found some _____ inside a small box. There were gold coins and jewellery.
   A kings   **B** treasure   **C** battles
5 The _____ of Hastings happened in 1066. The fighting was between the French and the English.
   A King   **B** Castle   **C** Battle
6 Big ships make a _____ noise when they come into the port.
   A clean   **B** light   **C** loud

GRAMMAR

1 **Choose the correct words.**

1 The ship *who/that* took Columbus to America in 1492 was called the *Santa Maria*.

2 That's the man *which/who* drives our school bus.

3 My granddad's got a motorbike *which/who* is 85 years old.

4 Alice is the girl *which/who* found the Roman treasure.

5 My mum works in a shop *who/that* sells bicycles.

6 These are the people *which/who* arrived on the ferry yesterday.

2 **Complete the sentences. Use the past simple or past continuous form of the verbs in brackets.**

1 We *were sailing* (sail) to the island when my hat *fell* (fall) into the sea.

2 The train _____ (leave) the station when Jacob _____ (arrive).

3 Emma and Nathan _____ (go) to school when the tram suddenly _____ (stop).

4 Lucy _____ (get off) the ferry when she _____ (see) me.

5 I _____ (travel) around Greece in a yacht when I _____ (meet) George and Maria.

6 We _____ (play) football in the park when we _____ (hear) the helicopter.

3 **Complete the short answers.**

1 Are you catching the coach tonight?
No, I _'m not_ .

2 Is Tom's class studying Ancient Greece next term?
Yes, it _____ .

3 Will you call me when you arrive?
Yes, I _____ .

4 Are they looking for treasure?
Yes, they _____ .

5 Is Paul going to be late?
No, he _____ .

6 Will his daughter become queen?
Yes, she _____ .

4 **Complete the conversation with one word in each space.**

William

Hurry up! The train 1) ___*is*___ leaving in 20 minutes and it 2) _____ take us 15 minutes to walk to the station.

Isobel

OK, OK! 3) _____ you taking your sunglasses with you?

William

Yes, it's 4) _____ to be hot and sunny today.

Isobel

Oh, great! I 5) _____ bring some sun cream, too. Are we going 6) _____ have a picnic at the castle?

William

No, we'll buy lunch at the café there.

Isobel

How 7) _____ we get from the station to the castle?

William

On foot, it's not far. Anyway, we 8) _____ going to be late, come on.

Isobel

All right. I'm ready now!

33

07 You can do it!

VOCABULARY

1 Find and write six sports.

g	i	n	f	o	n	s	t	e	s	a	g
s	h	o	r	s	e	r	i	d	i	n	g
o	n	t	i	n	g	d	i	d	i	n	b
n	t	o	g	f	d	e	s	d	i	n	a
p	e	n	t	s	w	e	r	o	k	i	s
l	n	a	i	e	n	a	o	j	o	o	k
g	n	i	n	n	o	n	b	u	s	h	e
s	i	n	t	b	e	e	n	d	o	n	t
i	s	w	e	r	e	d	i	o	n	a	b
s	a	t	b	a	l	i	s	k	o	l	a
a	i	n	r	u	n	n	i	n	g	x	l
k	o	n	b	a	s	k	y	b	a	i	l

1 _horse-riding_   2 ....
3 ....   4 ....
5 ....   6 ....

2 Choose the correct answer, A, B or C.

1 Why have you got that racket with you?
   A I've got a tennis lesson after school. *(circled)*
   B I'm playing in a basketball match later.
   C I'm going swimming with my sister.

2 Have you got any goggles I can borrow?
   A No, sorry, I don't play football.
   B Yes, I'll bring them to the swimming pool.
   C Yes, I have to wear them for gymnastics.

3 Isn't it a bit cold for surfing today, Jane?
   A Don't worry, Mum, I'll wear goggles.
   B Don't worry, Mum, I'll wear a swimsuit.
   C Don't worry, Mum, I'll wear a wetsuit.

4 Why can't we play volleyball today?
   A The board's broken.
   B The net's broken.
   C The helmet's broken.

5 Is that a new board, Gina?
   A Yes, I'm going to the gym now.
   B Yes, I'm going to the swimming pool now.
   C Yes, I'm going to the skateboarding park now.

6 Can I go horse-riding with Ella, Mum?
   A OK, but don't forget your helmet.
   B OK, but don't forget your ball.
   C OK, but don't forget your net.

3 Complete the sentences. Use the correct form of these expressions.

> do synchronised swimming   ~~play football~~
> go cycling   go skiing   do gymnastics
> play volleyball

1 She _plays football._   2 He ....

3 She ....   4 He ....

5 She ....   6 He ....

4 Choose the correct words.

1 Nick *plays/does* judo every Tuesday after school.
2 I *played/did* volleyball on the beach with my friends at the weekend.
3 Do you want to *go/do* gymnastics or go on the sports field?
4 I'm *doing/going* surfing with my sister after lunch.
5 My dad *goes/plays* running every morning at 6.30.
6 We *played/went* horse-riding when we were on holiday.
7 Kelly *goes/plays* skateboarding in the park at the weekends.
8 They're going to *go/play* basketball at school tomorrow.

5 Complete the advert with the correct words.

Archway Activity Centre
We have an activity for everyone here at Archway.

For people who like the outdoors, we have
1) _horse-riding_ for all levels and ages.
There are also lots of team games such as
football and 2) _____ .
Other outdoor activities include
3) _____ ,
4) _____ and
5) _____ .
When the weather is bad, we have great indoor activities to offer.
Why not try 6) _____ or
7) _____ ?

Our teachers are friendly and helpful.

We hope to see you soon at Archway!

See our website for more information – www.archway.activity.centre.

6 Complete the table with the correct verbs.

cycling	1)	_cycle_
skiing	2)	
surfing	3)	
skateboarding	4)	
running	5)	
swimming	6)	
climbing	7)	

7 Complete the sentences with these words.

~~climbed~~ cycle ran skied
surfed swam

1 We had lunch after we _climbed_ to the top of the rock.
2 They took their boards to the beach and _____ all morning.
3 Now I have a new bike I _____ to school every morning.
4 Robbie _____ from the boat to the island.
5 Chloe _____ the fastest and won the 100 m race.
6 We _____ really fast down the mountain – it was great fun!

8 Choose the correct words.

Hi Marta
My school is great for sports. Every week we have two PE lessons. In the summer, we usually
1) *go/play* tennis and volleyball. In the winter, we often 2) *play/do* gymnastics. There are also lots of after-school clubs. On Mondays there is volleyball
3) *practice/play* and on Tuesday there is a
4) *basketball/swimming* club at the local pool.
I go to the football club on Wednesdays. I
5) *do/play* for the school girls' football team. Every year we have a skiing trip to France. I went last year and 6) *skiing/skied* for the first time – I loved it! Our history teacher 7) *does/plays* judo and he's going to start a club next month. I really want to go to that club.
Love, Kim x

GRAMMAR
Ability, possibility and obligation: *could, can / can't, have to / don't have to*

1 Complete the sentences. Use *can* or *can't* and the verb in brackets.

1 Ruby _can't swim_ (swim). She's afraid of water.
2 My parents _____ (ride) a bike. They go cycling in the mountains.
3 Mark and Karen _____ (surf). They take their boards to the beach every weekend.
4 I _____ (skateboard). I tried it once, but I fell off all the time. I didn't enjoy it.
5 Lily _____ (run) very fast. She won a competition last month.
6 William _____ (play) tennis. He started lessons when he was just six years old.

2 Make questions with *can*. Then complete the short answers.

1 Mark / play / volleyball / ?
_____ Can Mark play volleyball? _____
Yes, _____ he can. _____
2 you / do / gymnastics / ?
_____
No, _____
3 your sister / ski / ?
_____
Yes, _____
4 Amelia and Eve / swim / ?
_____
Yes, _____
5 Max / ride / bike / ?
_____
No, _____
6 your parents / skateboard / ?
_____
No, _____

3 Complete the sentences with *can, can't, could* or *couldn't*.

Harriet: I remember the first time I went surfing. I
1) _couldn't_ stay on the board!
2) _____ you surf?
Ben: Yes, I 3) _____ . I go surfing with my brothers in the summer.
Jane: 4) _____ you play tennis when you were five?
Liam: No, I 5) _____ , but I learnt to play when I was seven.
Dean: 6) _____ you ski, Nick?
Nick: No, I 7) _____ , but I'm going for the first time this December. I 8) _____ skateboard so I think it will be easy to learn.

4 Complete the text with the best answer, A, B or C, for each space.

Racing Club
Tuesdays, 4.30 p.m. @ the race track

1) _____ you ride a bike? Do you enjoy cycling 2) _____ ? Then why not join our club?

You 3) _____ wear special clothing, just something warm and some trainers.
You 4) _____ wear a helmet because it 5) _____ be dangerous.

Racing club is £3 a week but you 6) _____ come the first week for free.

We hope to see you soon!

*You 7) _____ be over 14 years old to join the club.

1 A Could   (B) Can   C Can't
2 A fast   B faster   C fastest
3 A don't have to
  B didn't have to
  C doesn't have to
4 A had to   B has to   C have to
5 A can   B can't   C couldn't
6 A can't   B couldn't   C can
7 A have to   B has to   C had to

5 Complete the sentences with *have to/has to* or *don't have to/doesn't have to*.

1 Rebecca ___*has to*___ wear a helmet when she goes horse-riding.
2 You _____ wear goggles when you go skiing, but it's a good idea.
3 Tom _____ miss basketball practice today because he's ill.
4 We _____ do gymnastics at school, but I choose to do it.
5 Sometimes they _____ finish tennis matches early because of rain.
6 Mathew and Clara _____ cycle to school because their mum doesn't have a car.

6 Match the questions (1–6) with the answers (A–F).

1 Do we have to wear goggles in the pool? _F_
2 Did Aaron have to play in the basketball match?
3 Does everyone have to wear a cycling helmet?
4 Can your mum ski well?
5 Do I have to wear trainers for judo?
6 Could Mark kiteboard last summer?

A Yes, he did. The team captain was sick.
B Yes, she can. She won lots of skiing competitions when she was young.
C No, you don't. You don't wear anything on your feet.
D Yes, they do. It can be dangerous when they're cycling very fast.
E No, he couldn't. He only learnt to do it this year.
F No, you don't have to, but the water can make your eyes red.

7 Complete the text with one word in each space.

Local girl number 1 in gymnastics competition!

Samantha Combe is a very happy 14-year-old. Yesterday, she won a national gymnastics competition. She 1) ___*had*___ to practise very hard for the competition. Every day she had to 2) _____ four hours of gymnastics. She didn't have 3) _____ go far to practise – Samantha lives next door to the gym! The competition was very difficult and she 4) _____ to beat ten other girls to win first prize. Today Samantha is relaxing at home with a DVD. She 5) _____ have to practise for a few days so she 6) _____ have a rest!

Adverbs

8 Complete the sentences with adverbs formed from the adjectives in brackets.

1 He plays tennis ___*well*___ . (good)
2 Clare runs _____ . (fast)
3 David always arrives _____ . (late)
4 I play football _____ . (bad)
5 She won the race _____ . (easy)
6 She climbed up the mountain _____ . (slow)

See the world

VOCABULARY

1 Find and write the names of eight animals.

s	u	o	m	o	o	n	s	t	z
t	g	r	o	e	h	a	n	d	a
a	i	e	u	z	e	a	a	a	r
k	r	e	s	n	h	i	k	e	d
e	a	n	e	p	d	e	e	t	y
e	f	f	e	r	i	g	r	i	f
t	f	l	o	n	e	d	i	g	s
l	e	o	p	a	r	d	e	e	x
u	d	o	r	i	z	e	b	r	a
n	g	u	l	e	b	r	i	d	e

1	*mouse*	2	
3		4	
5		6	
7		8	

2 Find and write six adjectives.

asddsfdifficultaseddgreatasddfunasssspsascaryasapdexcitingasddlonelydsdfg

1	*difficult*	2	
3		4	
5		6	

3 Choose the correct words.

1 How was your elephant ride?
Great!/*Scary*! I loved it. The elephant was very friendly and gentle.

2 Did you finish your homework about spiders?
Not all of it. I found it really *difficult/lonely*.

3 What did you think of the safari?
It was really *lonely/exciting* and my friends loved it, too.

4 Do you enjoy filming leopards in China?
Yes, I do, but it can be *fun/lonely* sometimes and I miss my family.

5 Was your trip to the zoo *difficult/fun*?
Yes, we really enjoyed it.

6 Why don't you like spiders? They're really cute!
No, they're not! They're really *scary/great*!

4 Choose the correct words or phrases.

1 It was *freezing cold*/*cool* yesterday. It was –3°C when we walked to school!

2 We'd like a *hot/cool* drink, please. It's boiling hot outside!

3 Would you like another blanket or are you *warm/cold* enough?

4 Don't touch the water, it's *warm/boiling hot*. You'll hurt your hand.

5 We'll have *cold/cool* food at the party. I'll make some salads and sandwiches.

6 It's very *hot/cool* in here. Can we open a window, please?

5 Complete the sentences with the correct weather adjectives.

cloudy   foggy   ~~rainy~~   snowy   stormy   sunny   windy

1 I always take my umbrella when it's ___*rainy*___.

2 When it's very _____ we go skiing in the mountains.

3 It's a really _____ day. Let's go to the beach!

4 Why are you wearing sunglasses? It's _____ .

5 It's very _____ . It's great weather for flying kites!

6 We can't sail our boat when it's _____ . It's too dangerous.

7 They can't see the top of the mountain because it's _____ .

6 **Test your geography! Match the places (1–7) with the correct continents (a–g).**

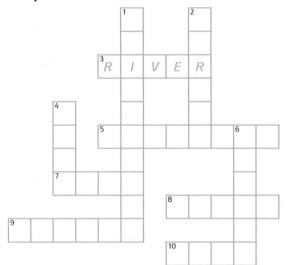

1	Brazil	**a**	Asia
2	Egypt	**b**	Europe
3	Canada	**c**	South America
4	China	**d**	Antarctica
5	The South Pole	**e**	Australia
6	New Zealand	**f**	Africa
7	Poland	**g**	North America

7 **Complete the crossword.**

Across

3 water that travels across land to the sea

5 a very high area of land

7 a large area of water that has land all around it

8 a very large sea

9 a very dry place with lots of sand

10 a small area with trees

Down

1 a place with lots of very tall trees where it often rains

2 a place with lots of trees

4 a high area of land smaller than 5 across

6 a place with water all around it

8 **Complete the sentences with these measurements.**

53 kg   6,650 km   8 cm   2 °C̶   300 kg

1 It's only _____2 °C_____ . It's very cold today.

2 The River Nile is _____ long.

3 This Siberian tiger weighs _____ .

4 My pet mouse is _____ long.

5 My friend Joshua weighs _____ .

9 **Complete the conversation with these words.**

Asia   continents   spring   summer   temperature   weather   winter   wo̶r̶l̶d̶

Martin: Hi. I'm Martin from *Teen Travel* magazine and we're talking to teenagers from different cities around the 1) _____world_____ . What's your name and where do you come from?

Leyla: Hi. I'm Leyla and I come from Istanbul in Turkey.

Martin: So what's interesting about your city?

Leyla: Well, Istanbul's unusual because it's in two 2) _____ . The old part of the city is in Europe and the new part of the city is in 3) _____ .

Martin: That is unusual! What's the 4) _____ like in your city?

Leyla: It changes at different times of the year. In Istanbul 5) _____ starts in June and finishes in September. July is usually the warmest month. The 6) _____ once reached 37 °C, but it isn't usually that hot. It's normally around 28 °C.

Martin: And does it get cold in Istanbul?

Leyla: It doesn't really start to get cold until the middle of December. It usually snows in 7) _____ . The weather starts to get warmer again in March when 8) _____ starts.

GRAMMAR
Present perfect simple

1 Complete the sentences with the correct form of *have*. Use the contractions *'ve*/*'s* where possible.

1 **Joel:** Did you enjoy your trip to Venezuela?
  Connie: Yes, we loved it.
  Joel: Was it your first trip to South America?
  Connie: No, we _'ve_ been there before.

2 **Dad:** How do you know so much about the South Pole, Kerry?
  Kerry: We _____ read lots of books about Antarctica at school, Dad.

3 **Sara:** How did you find this beach? It's amazing!
  Anna: Mark and Kerry _____ been here before. They told me about it.

4 **Mark:** Does Richard know lots of people here?
  Noah: Yes, he _____ visited this island many times. A lot of people on the island know him now.

5 **William:** Do you like mountain climbing?
  Olivia: I love it! I _____ climbed the highest mountain in my country.

6 **Kate:** Where is Andrea going next month?
  Nick: Kenya and Tanzania. She _____ travelled to Asia and Europe and now she wants to go to Africa.

2 Put the words in the correct order to make negative sentences and questions.

1 hasn't / Jacob / my pet snake / seen / .
  Jacob hasn't seen my pet snake.

2 a zoo / you / Have / been / ever / to/ ?
  ....

3 never / by boat / travelled / We've / .
  ....

4 ever / to Tokyo / Charlotte / Has / been / ?
  ....

5 a holiday / They / had / in the UK / haven't / .
  ....

6 it / here / Has / snowed / ever / ?
  ....

7 never / mountain climbing / I've / liked / .
  ....

3 Complete the table with the past participles of the verbs.

go	1)	_been/gone_
see	2)	
take	3)	
buy	4)	
read	5)	
catch	6)	
teach	7)	

4 Complete the sentences with the present perfect form of the verbs in brackets.

1 Eric _has stayed_ (stay) in many places in Thailand.
2 Jimmy and Didier _____ (see) a tiger in the wild.
3 Harriet _____ (not be) to Europe before.
4 This is the first time it _____ (snow) here.
5 We _____ (not buy) our tickets to Italy yet.
6 I _____ (not hold) a snake before.

5 Complete the short answers.

1 Have you ever been to Australia?
  No, _I haven't_ .
2 Has Tracy read the book about Antarctica?
  Yes, _____ .
3 Have they camped in a desert before?
  No, _____ .
4 Has it snowed here before?
  No, _____ .
5 Have Ben and Kerry skied in these mountains?
  Yes, _____ .
6 Has your granddad ever lived on another continent?
  Yes, _____ .

Using *ever* and *never* with the present perfect

6 Make questions. Use the present perfect with *ever*.

1 you / see / a black widow spider / ?

   Have you ever seen a black widow spider?

2 your teacher / go / to the Amazon / ?

3 your parents / go / mountain climbing / ?

4 Georgina / sleep / in a rainforest / ?

5 they / find / a mouse in their house / ?

6 Martin / visit / the island of Corsica / ?

7 Make sentences with *never*. Use the present perfect form of these verbs.

| climb   live   rain   ride   see   ~~swim~~ |

1 Mark *has never swum* in an ocean.
2 Susan and Matthew _____ a mountain.
3 It _____ in this part of the desert.
4 My sister _____ on an elephant, but it's something she really wants to do.
5 This snake _____ in the wild. It was born in the zoo.
6 Lucien _____ fog before. They don't have fog in his country.

8 Complete the text with the best answer, A, B or C, in each space.

Adventureholiday4u.com

Katie is a lucky 14-year-old. She has 1) _____ all over the world with her parents, Mandy and Tom. We asked Katie to talk to us about some of her adventure holidays.

— How many adventure holidays 2) _____ you been on?

— Six. I 3) _____ on my first adventure holiday when I was seven.

— Wow! Have you got a favourite holiday?

— Not really. I've 4) _____ all the holidays. I love animals so our last holiday was fantastic — we went on safari in Tanzania.

— Have you 5) _____ had a scary experience on one of your adventure holidays?

— Yes. When we were on safari in Tanzania an elephant ran towards our jeep. That was scary, but also amazing!

— What kinds of sports or activities have you 6) _____ on holiday?

— Well, my family loves extreme sports. We've been ice climbing in Canada, snowboarding in the desert in Dubai and surfing in Australia.

— Fantastic! So why do you like adventure holidays so much?

— You're never bored! I've 7) _____ lots of amazing places and done brilliant things on my holidays. I've 8) _____ been on a beach holiday — and I don't want to! I love adventure holidays!

1	A travelling	(B) travelled	C travels
2	A have	B has	C had
3	A go	B went	C gone
4	A enjoy	B enjoying	C enjoyed
5	A ever	B never	C not
6	A do	B did	C done
7	A see	B seen	C saw
8	A ever	B never	C not

Revision Units 7 – 8

VOCABULARY

1 Choose the correct words.

1 Have you ever *played*/*been* volleyball on a beach?
2 Has Andrew ever *been*/*played* cycling with you?
3 Have you ever *done*/*been* gymnastics at school?
4 Has Sarah ever *played*/*done* synchronised swimming?
5 Has Michael ever *been*/*played* skiing in France?
6 Has Simon ever *done*/*played* football for the school team?

2 Choose the correct words.

1 Martin swam to the other side of the *lake*/*ocean* really fast.
2 We love playing in the *rainforest*/*wood* near our house. It's great in the winter when it snows.
3 I'm really good at running. I can run up that *mountain*/*hill* in ten minutes.
4 We always go to this *island*/*desert* on holiday. It's always hot and sunny and it's so green.
5 I've never been to the top of a *forest*/*mountain* because I don't like heights.
6 Juliette and her dad like going fishing in the *river*/*island*.

3 Complete the sentences with these words.

> board   ~~goggles~~   helmet   net   rackets
> swimsuits

1 *Goggles* can help you see better when you swim underwater.
2 Do you want to go surfing? You don't need to have your own _____ .
3 Do you want to play tennis? I've got two _____ .
4 It's so hot and sunny. Let's put on our _____ and go to the beach.
5 Cycling in the mountains can be dangerous so you have to wear a _____ .
6 The volleyball _____ has a big hole in it. Can you fix it for us, please?

4 Complete the conversation with these words.

> cool   fast   ~~freezing~~   kiteboarding
> snow   sunny   wetsuits   windy

Daniel
Hi, Maria. How was your trip to the mountains?

Maria
Good, thanks. It was
1) *freezing* cold, though!

Daniel
Did it 2) _____ ?

Maria
Yes, a lot. We went skiing every day. How about your trip? Where did you go?

Daniel
Crete, in Greece. It was great. It was really 3) _____ .

Maria
Did you go in the sea?

Daniel
Yes, but the water was a bit 4) _____ so we wore 5) _____ . We also tried 6) _____ on the beach.

Maria
Wow! I've never done that.

Daniel
It was my first time. It was very 7) _____ so we went really 8) _____ . It was great!

GRAMMAR

1 **Complete the sentences with adverbs formed from the adjectives in brackets.**

1 The giraffes moved _____slowly_____ in the hot weather. (slow)

2 The elephant hurt its foot and was walking _____. (bad)

3 We couldn't hear the snake. It moved _____ through the rainforest. (quiet)

4 The mouse escaped _____ through the small hole in the wall. (easy)

5 Leopards are good at climbing. They can climb trees really _____. (good)

6 Tigers can run very _____ – often 35 miles an hour. (fast)

2 **Complete the conversations with the present perfect form of these verbs.**

> climb ~~cycle~~ go run skateboard
> wear

1 _____Have_____ you ever _____cycled_____ through a forest?
Yes, I have. I took my bike when I visited Sherwood Forest.

2 _____ Mark ever _____ a tree?
Yes, he has. When he was young he had a tree house.

3 _____ your dad ever _____?
Yes, he has. He tried on my board, but he fell off lots of times!

4 _____ they ever _____ to Africa?
Yes, they have. They went to Morocco last September.

5 _____ you ever _____ a wetsuit?
Yes, I have. I went surfing in the UK and the sea was freezing cold!

6 _____ Rachel ever _____ in a race?
Yes, she has. She did the New York marathon last year. Her feet really hurt afterwards!

3 **Choose the correct answer, A, B or C.**

1 Jake _____ when he started at our school, but now he's a really good swimmer.
A had to swim
B couldn't swim
C has swum

2 David _____ snow before. He comes from Botswana in Africa.
A has never seen
B can see
C has to see

3 You _____ lessons to learn how to surf, but it's a good idea.
A can't take
B don't have to take
C couldn't take

4 Horse-riding _____ dangerous so I always wear a helmet.
A can be
B has to be
C couldn't be

5 I _____ to Europe, but I would like to go one day.
A could be
B had to be
C haven't been

6 We _____ tennis at the moment because there isn't a net.
A can't play
B have to play
C have played

4 **Complete the conversation. Use one word in each space.**

Paul: Have you 1) _____ever_____ been to Blackwood Activity Centre?

Holly: 2) _____, I haven't. What can you do there?

Paul: Lots of things. You 3) _____ do horse-riding, kiteboarding, rock climbing and judo.

Holly: So, 4) _____ you been there?

Paul: Yes, I went last Saturday.

Holly: What 5) _____ you do?

Paul: I wanted to go kiteboarding, but we couldn't because it was too windy.

Holly: I thought it has 6) _____ be windy for kiteboarding.

Paul: It does, but when it's very windy it can 7) _____ dangerous. I did judo instead – I really enjoyed it.

Holly: Yes, I love judo. I go to a judo club at the sports centre.

Paul: 8) _____ you have to be good to join the club?

Holly: No, you don't. Why don't you come with me next time?

Let me entertain you

VOCABULARY

1 Match the types of TV shows (1–6) with the programmes (A–F) in the TV guide.

1 talent show — _B_
2 chat show — _____
3 news programme — _____
4 documentary — _____
5 soap opera — _____
6 sports programme — _____

19.00	**A Cat watch** Michelle Oldfield follows a family of tigers in Cambodia.
19.30	**B Star lights** Who will win the competition? Will it be Sandy the magician, Denzel the singer or the dancing group Fire? Find out tonight.
20.30	**C Harvey Street** In tonight's episode, find out whether Amy left Mark – and is Robert telling the truth about the accident?
21.00	**D Points East** Find out what's happening in your area.
21.15	**E Talk with Tina** The actor Mark Robson is a guest on Tina's show tonight. He will talk about his new film.
22.00	**F Match Round Up** All the results from today's matches and races.

2 Complete the sentences.

1 An _actor_ is someone who acts.
2 A _____ is someone who dances.
3 A _____ is someone who sings.
4 A _____ is someone who does magic tricks.
5 A _____ is someone who plays music.
6 A _____ is someone who performs comedy.

3 Choose the correct words.

1 My sister loves _soap operas/sports programmes_. Her favourite is about a family called the Fletchers.
2 I love singing and dancing. One day I want to go on a _documentary/talent show_.
3 Some actors are very private and they never go on _chat shows/sports programmes_.
4 My dad's on the _sports programme/news programme_ at 6 o'clock. They interviewed him about his business.
5 My brother watches a _sports programme/chat show_ every Saturday evening. He's mad about football.
6 I saw a really interesting _documentary/soap opera_ about Machu Picchu last night.

4 Put the letters in order to make different types of films.

1 icatno ilmf — _action film_
2 niomaatin — _____
3 odcyme — _____
4 oorrrh lfmi — _____
5 mcraonti mfli — _____
6 icseenc iftcnio ifml — _____

5 Choose the correct words.

1 I love this _romantic/science fiction_ film. It's about a man who saves the world from aliens.
2 This _horror film/comedy_ is really funny. You won't stop laughing!
3 I'm not interested in _action/comedy_ films. They're full of fighting and fast cars.
4 My brother doesn't like _romantic/action_ films. He doesn't like any films about love.
5 This _animation/horror film_ is about the characters from my favourite comic. It's great fun!
6 I don't like watching _romantic/horror_ films before I go to sleep because they give me scary dreams.

6 **Find and write six adjectives to describe films or TV shows.**

b	o	r	i	n	f	s	c	a	s
i	n	g	n	i	g	u	n	k	c
n	o	l	t	e	r	e	n	s	a
g	i	s	e	l	l	i	o	n	r
o	b	o	r	i	n	g	k	r	y
n	g	n	e	t	r	s	i	o	n
r	i	d	s	t	r	a	n	g	e
o	u	s	t	c	a	n	y	o	u
r	i	d	i	c	u	l	o	u	s
f	u	i	n	t	e	r	i	n	g
y	a	r	g	o	g	e	t	s	o

1 _____ *scary*
2 _____
3 _____
4 _____
5 _____
6 _____

7 **Choose the best answer, A, B or C.**

1 We saw a really _____ comedian on TV last night. We couldn't stop laughing.
   A scary   **B** boring   **C** funny

2 Harry is a great _____ . He can play the guitar and the drums.
   A magician   **B** musician   **C** singer

3 The magician was wearing a _____ hat with a pineapple on top of it!
   A ridiculous   **B** scary   **C** boring

4 Tom's a great _____ . He was in a really scary horror film.
   A comedian   **B** magician   **C** actor

5 Did you watch that _____ 'Gold'? I think the stories are always ridiculous.
   A news programme
   B soap opera
   C talent show

6 The Great Alfonso was a famous _____ . He did some brilliant card tricks.
   A magician   **B** dancer   **C** singer

8 **Complete the text with these words.**

audience   comedian   contestants
judges   show   stage   ~~talent show~~   TV

Reach for the Stars! is a new
1) _talent show_ that is starting on Channel 9 next week. There are many talent shows on
2) _____ , but this one is different as it is only for teenagers. All the 3) _____ are between 14 and 19 years old. They will perform on 4) _____ in front of four 5) _____ who will be a dancer, a singer, a 6) _____ and a magician. The judges will give the contestants marks out of ten, but the 7) _____ will decide which contestant leaves the 8) _____ each week. It starts next Thursday. Don't miss it!

GRAMMAR
Present perfect with *for* and *since*

1 Put the words in the correct order to make sentences.

1 played / Cathy / in the band / for six months / has / .

   Cathy has played in the band for six months.

2 since 1988 / has / on TV / been / This soap opera / .

3 loved / since she was a small child / ballet dancing / has / Michaela / .

4 have / for two years / had / Theo and Robin / singing lessons / .

5 played / since I was eight years old / 've / the violin / I / .

6 our drama teacher / known / We / for a long time / 've / .

2 Choose the correct word, *for* or *since*.

1 *for*/*since* this morning
2 *for*/*since* three hours
3 *for*/*since* ages
4 *for*/*since* yesterday
5 *for*/*since* twelve weeks
6 *for*/*since* 1931
7 *for*/*since* the twelfth century
8 *for*/*since* a few minutes

3 Choose the correct words.

1 We've been here *since*/*for* 3 o'clock.
2 Maria Cohen has appeared in this soap opera *since*/*for* thirteen years.
3 My cousin's been a professional ballet dancer *since*/*for* she was sixteen.
4 I've been interested in magic *since*/*for* I was a small child.
5 Colette has been a musician *since*/*for* a long time.
6 They have won lots of talent competitions *since*/*for* they started their band.

4 Complete the sentences. Use the present perfect form of the verbs in brackets and *for* or *since*.

1 Sara ___*has had*___ her guitar ___*since*___ her thirteenth birthday. (have)
2 I _____ to the cinema _____ a long time. (not be)
3 Joe _____ as a professional clown _____ ten years. (work)
4 Diane _____ that actor _____ his first film in 2007. (love)
5 They _____ each other _____ years. (know)
6 Rosie _____ her friend Scott _____ he joined the ballet. (not see)

5 Make questions. Use the present perfect with *how long*.

1 you / know / Joanna and Faye / ?

   How long have you known Joanna and Faye?

2 you / be / at this drama college / ?

3 Jack / want / to be an actor / ?

4 Yasmin / have / this talent / ?

5 your dad / play / the piano / ?

6 they / live / in Hollywood / ?

6 Complete the interview. Use one word in each
space.

Sandy

Hi, sorry I'm late. How 1) _____*long*_____
have you been here?

Interviewer

I 2) _____ only been here for five minutes,
don't worry. So, Sandy, 3) _____ long have
you been in the group 'The Hot Heads'?

Sandy

4) _____ last July, but I've known the
others in the group 5) _____ a long time.

Interviewer

So what made you start your own group?

Sandy

Well, we 6) _____ been
interested in music for years and
always wanted to play in a band.

Interviewer

Right, and you play lead guitar, Sandy?

Sandy

Yes, I've 7) _____ the guitar
since I was about six. My dad
taught me how to play.

Interviewer

And you won a national
talent competition recently?

Sandy

Yes, that was amazing. We've won three
competitions 8) _____ we started
the band, but that was the biggest.

Interviewer

Well, I wish you lots of luck for
your future music career!

Sandy

Thank you.

Present perfect with *just*

7 Make sentences. Use the present perfect with
just.

1 Kathy / send / an email to Pete.
   Kathy's just sent an email to Pete.

2 I / start / a great book.
   _____

3 They / choose / the winner.
   _____

4 The magician / arrive / on stage.
   _____

5 Danny / appear / in a new film.
   _____

6 She / join / a rock band.
   _____

8 Complete the short conversations. Use *just* and
the present perfect form of these verbs.

> buy   finish   ~~leave~~   phone   see   tell

1 Where's Ben, Mum?
   He's at his music club. He *'s just left* to catch a bus.

2 What are you laughing at?
   This comedian on TV. He _____ the funniest
   joke!

3 Where are you going?
   To the cinema. Jake _____ and he's got
   some free tickets.

4 What's in that bag?
   New ballet shoes – I _____ them. Do you
   want to have a look?

5 What's the matter, Sophie?
   I wanted to watch my favourite soap opera on TV
   and it _____ .

6 Dad, do you know where my new DVD is?
   Yes, it's on the kitchen table, I _____ it.

10 Eat well, feel well

VOCABULARY

1 Look at the pictures and complete the sentences with the correct form of these verbs.

~~bake~~ barbecue boil fry grill roast

1 Noah _____baked_____ some bread at school yesterday.

2 Can you _____ some water for the vegetables, please?

3 My dad enjoys _____ in the summer.

4 Mum's in the kitchen at the moment. She _____ a chicken for dinner.

5 We always _____ our meat. It's healthier that way.

6 I _____ the chicken for the salad this morning.

2 Complete the sentences with adjectives formed from the verbs in brackets.

1 My parents had ___grilled___ fish and salad for lunch. (grill)
2 I love the smell of freshly _____ bread. (bake)
3 My brother hates _____ eggs. (fry)
4 We all love _____ food in our family. (barbecue)
5 My grandma always gives us meat and _____ vegetables for dinner. (boil)
6 I love my mum's _____ potatoes. (roast)

3 Complete the table with these words.

~~chips~~ chocolate crisps ice cream lemon lime

sweet	salty	sour
	chips	

4 Choose the correct words.

1 I have to do regular *exercise*/*fit* now I'm in the basketball team.
2 I love *junk food*/*snacks*. My favourite is hamburger and fries.
3 Driving everywhere can be *unfit*/*unhealthy*. It's a good idea to walk more.
4 It's *fit*/*healthy* to do twenty minutes of exercise three times a week.
5 At school we have fruit for a *snack*/*meal* at morning break.
6 Sophie is very *fit*/*unhealthy*. She can run up the hill in five minutes!

5 Complete the email with these words.

do   ~~fit~~   healthy   junk   regular   unfit

Hi, Robbie

Do you still go to the gym? I want to get
1) _____fit_____ because I'd like to join the school
volleyball team. I've stopped eating 2) _____
food and I eat lots of 3) _____ food like fruit
and vegetables. I'm not very 4) _____ , but
it's been a long time since I played any sport. I
need to start doing some 5) _____ exercise
soon. They'll choose the players for the volleyball
team next month. What kind of exercise do you
6) _____ ?

Can you help me?

Thanks.

Jennie

6 Add *i, e, a, o* or *u* to make nouns about not feeling well.

1 c_o_ld
2 h_____d_ch_____
3 s_____r_____ thr_____t
4 c_____gh
5 st_____m_____ch _____ch_____
6 t_____mp_____r_____t_____r
7 t_____th_____ch_____

7 Choose the correct answer, A, B or C.

1 Are you OK, Jacob? Your eyes and nose are red.

I've got a _____ . I feel terrible!

A toothache
Ⓑ cold
C stomach ache

2 Do you want some of this chocolate cake?

I can't. I've got really bad _____ and it hurts when
I eat.

A temperature
B headache
C toothache

3 Why are you wearing that thick scarf, Rosie?

I've got a _____ and it feels better when my
neck's warm.

A sore throat
B temperature
C stomach ache

4 Have I got a _____ ?

Yes, it's 39°C. You're very hot. I'll give you some
medicine.

A temperature
B toothache
C cough

5 Your _____ sounds bad! Do you want a glass of
water?

I'm OK, thanks. It happens every time I speak.
I think I need to go to the doctor's.

A toothache
B cough
C stomach ache

6 Why have you got your eyes closed?

I've got a bad _____ and the light makes it feel
worse.

A headache
B sore throat
C cough

8 Complete the email with these words.

barbecue   exercise   ~~fitter~~   food   fried
sweet   vegetables

Hi, Yan

We've got a new basketball teacher and he's
given us a training programme. He says it will
make us 1) _____fitter_____ and healthier. I hope it
makes us win some more basketball matches, too!
The training programme tells us how much
2) _____ we need to do every week and
also what 3) _____ to eat. I need to eat five
types of fruit or 4) _____ a day. I should only
grill or 5) _____ meat. I shouldn't eat any
6) _____ food – which means no junk food!
I also shouldn't eat too much 7) _____ food,
like biscuits. I only started it yesterday so I will tell
you how it goes!

Callum

GRAMMAR
Obligation and prohibition

1 **Choose the correct words.**

1 You *must/mustn't* cook chicken well before you eat it.

2 I *must/mustn't* check the cake in the oven. I think it's ready now.

3 You *must/mustn't* touch the oven. It's very hot.

4 Freddie has toothache and *must/mustn't* eat any sweets.

5 You *must/mustn't* forget to switch the oven off after you use it.

6 The children *must/mustn't* wash their hands before dinner.

2 **Complete the sentences with *must* or *mustn't* and these verbs.**

> bring   do   ~~eat~~   keep   remember   see

1 My mum says I _*mustn't eat*_ sweets before dinner.

2 You .... the milk in the fridge or it will go bad.

3 Athletes .... regular exercise.

4 You .... to drink lots of water when you do exercise.

5 Cara .... the dentist about her toothache.

6 You .... any food into the computer room.

3 **Complete the sentences with *must* or *mustn't*.**

1 You _*musn't*_ eat food here.

2 You .... wash your hands.

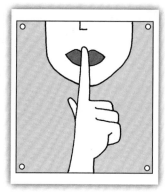

3 You .... play ball games here.

4 You .... be quiet.

5 You .... use your mobile phone.

6 You .... bring dogs here.

4 **Look at Joseph's list for his birthday party and complete the sentences with *needs to* and *doesn't need to*.**

Party - things to do!	Done
phone DJ	✓
buy cola and juice	
get some snacks	
invite friends	✓
buy new jeans	
borrow party lights from Gavin	✓

1 Joseph _*doesn't need to*_ phone the DJ.

2 Joseph .... buy cola and juice.

3 Joseph .... get some snacks.

4 Joseph .... invite his friends.

5 Joseph .... buy new jeans.

6 Joseph .... borrow party lights from Gavin.

5 Choose the correct words.

1 John _needs_/doesn't need to eat more fruit and vegetables. He doesn't eat enough healthy food.

2 I _don't need_/need a snack. I'm really hungry and I can't wait until dinner.

3 Kelly _doesn't need_/needs to do more exercise. She's very fit and plays lots of sports.

4 We _don't need_/need to fry the onions first. Then we add the chicken and peppers later.

5 You _need_/don't need to wash your hands before you prepare food.

6 You _don't need_/need to buy more juice. We have lots in the fridge.

7 Rob _needs_/doesn't need to go to the doctor's. He feels better now.

should

6 Complete the sentences. Use _should_ or _shouldn't_ and the verbs in brackets.

1 You look hot. You _should have_ (have) a cold drink.

2 Mark is very tired. He _____ (get) more sleep.

3 You _____ (ask) Sam to help you with your homework. He's good at maths.

4 Jack _____ (go) swimming today. He's got a bad cold.

5 Alice _____ (enter) a cooking competition. She's really good.

6 My dad _____ (put) so much salt on his food. It's very unhealthy.

7 William and Ben _____ (leave) home earlier. They're always late for school.

7 Choose the best answer, A, B or C.

1 I can't sleep because I've got a big exam tomorrow.
   A You shouldn't worry so much.
   B You must study more.
   C You don't have to sleep.

2 Do you want to come to the park with us?
   A I don't need to go. I'm meeting my mum.
   B I mustn't leave the park. I'm meeting my mum.
   C I'm meeting my mum and I mustn't be late.

3 Your cough is getting worse. I'll call the doctor.
   A Thanks, but you shouldn't. I've got an appointment for this afternoon.
   B Thanks, but you don't need to. I've got an appointment for this afternoon.
   C Thanks, but you must. I've got an appointment for this afternoon.

4 Are you ready for school?
   A Nearly. I just need to brush my teeth.
   B No, I shouldn't be ready in five minutes.
   C I mustn't be late for school.

5 Can I borrow your sports bag, Dan?
   A Yes, you should.
   B OK, but you must give it back to me.
   C You don't need to borrow it.

6 I want to get fit. What should I do?
   A You shouldn't do regular exercise.
   B You mustn't do regular exercise.
   C You need to do regular exercise.

8 Complete the text with the best answer, A, B or C, for each space.

Recipe for a great party!

■ You 1) _____ to invite a good group of friends. You can't have a good party without a good group of people.

■ Be careful how you invite your friends. You 2) _____ tell people about your party on a social networking site. You don't want hundreds of people to arrive at your party!

■ You 3) _____ make sure that everyone has enough to eat and drink.

■ Good music is very important. You 4) _____ to get a DJ, but you 5) _____ have a good variety of music to play.

■ Lastly, you 6) _____ forget to take some photos – they're a great way to remember the party!

	A	B	C
1	must	should	**need**
2	shouldn't	must	don't need
3	mustn't	should	need
4	don't need	shouldn't	mustn't
5	need	must	shouldn't
6	mustn't	don't need	should

Revision Units 9 – 10

VOCABULARY

1 Complete the conversations with these words.

> chat show   documentary
> ~~horror film~~   romantic films
> soap opera   sports programme

1 I really want to watch this _horror film_ – I love scary films.

Me too, but you need to be 18 to watch that film.

2 I love that new singer, Rocco. Have you heard him?

Yes, he's great. There's an interview with him on a ＿＿＿＿＿ tonight.

3 Have you heard of this ＿＿＿＿＿? It's called 'Hollywood Lights'.

Yes, it's great. It's about two rich families who are always fighting with each other.

4 Did you watch the football match this afternoon?

No, I didn't. I'm going to watch some of it on the ＿＿＿＿＿ later.

5 What's your sister watching?

It's a boring film about two people who fall in love. I hate ＿＿＿＿＿!

6 You should do your homework now, Luke.

I am, Mum. I'm watching this ＿＿＿＿＿ about mountains for geography.

2 Choose the correct words.

1 We're going to _bake_/boil some cakes at school tomorrow.

2 One of the healthiest ways to cook meat is to _fry/grill_ it.

3 Have you ever _barbecued/baked_ fish on a wood fire? It's really nice.

4 I love the smell of _roast/boiled_ chicken when it comes out of the oven.

5 Can you _boil/fry_ some water for the potatoes, please?

6 I've got some oil left in the pan. Would you like a _boiled/fried_ egg?

3 Complete the review of a TV programme with these words.

> audience   comedian   contestants
> funny   judges   show   ~~talent show~~   TV

The Great Cooking Contest

I love The Great Cooking Contest. It's like a 1) _talent show_ for teenage cooks. There are ten 2) ＿＿＿＿＿ and every week they have to cook different things. They do the cooking in a TV studio in front of an 3) ＿＿＿＿＿. At the end of the 4) ＿＿＿＿＿ they get marks for their cooking. There are four 5) ＿＿＿＿＿ who give marks. Three of them are famous chefs, but one judge is a 6) ＿＿＿＿＿. She's really 7) ＿＿＿＿＿. I think this is the best programme on 8) ＿＿＿＿＿!

4 Choose the correct words.

Alex: Hi, Harriet. Do you do 1) _fit/regular_ exercise?

Harriet: Yes, I go to the gym every week and play basketball on Tuesdays. Why?

Alex: I'm really 2) _unfit/junk_, but I don't know what to do.

Harriet: Why don't you join my gym? It's good fun. You also need to stop eating 3) _healthy/junk_ food like that burger you're eating now!

Alex: I know, but I love 4) _grilled/fried_ food!

Harriet: Well, you can still eat it sometimes, but you need to eat more 5) _healthy/boiled_ food.

Alex: Yes, you're right. Can I come with you next time you go to the gym? I haven't done any 6) _snacks/exercise_ for ages, so can you show me what to do?

Harriet: Yes, sure. I'll send you a text.

Alex: Thanks.

GRAMMAR

1 Complete these conversations with *just* and the present perfect form of the verbs in brackets.

1 What's the matter, Emily?

I _'ve just bitten_ (bite) into this orange and it's really sour!

2 Why isn't Danny eating any ice cream?

He _____ (come) back from the dentist and he's got toothache.

3 Something smells really nice. What is it?

My dad _____ (bake) some bread. We can have some for lunch.

4 I'm really hungry. Is there anything to eat?

I _____ (grill) some sausages. Do you want some in a sandwich?

5 Rebecca and Joe don't look very well. Are they all right?

They _____ (eat) two big pizzas and I think they've got stomach ache.

6 Do you want an orange juice?

No, thanks – I _____ (drink) a bottle of cola.

2 Choose the correct words.

> **Talent Show**
> **Saturday 12 March**
> **(13-17 yrs only)**

1 All talent show contestants *must/mustn't* be between 13 and 17 years old.

> **White chocolate biscuits**
> Baking time: 10 minutes at 180°C

2 You *don't need to/need to* bake these biscuits at 180°C.

> **Do not take more than 8 in 24 hours.**

3 You *should/mustn't* have more than eight sore throat sweets in a day.

> **Mayflower Singing Club**
> – all levels welcome!

4 You *need/don't need* to be a really good singer to join the singing club.

> **Adults:** 6 g of salt or less a day

5 Adults *must/shouldn't* eat more than 6 g of salt a day.

> **Please switch off your mobile phone.**

6 The audience *must/don't need to* switch off their mobile phones during the show.

3 Complete the sentences with *for* or *since*.

1 I haven't eaten chocolate cake ___*since*___ my birthday last year.

2 My brother's really fit. He's been in our school football team _____ three years.

3 I've had a headache _____ I woke up this morning.

4 This actor hasn't been in a film _____ 2012.

5 I haven't watched this soap opera _____ ages.

6 I haven't bought any junk food _____ the last two months. I'm trying to be healthy.

7 Tom's had a bad cough _____ Friday. I think he should see the doctor.

8 You only need to fry this fish _____ five minutes.

4 Complete these questions and answers with one word in each space.

1 How long have you been a magician?

___*Since*___ I was 13 years old.

2 Should I roast the vegetables at 180°C?

No, the oven needs _____ be hotter than that.

3 When will dinner be ready?

About 1 o'clock. I _____ just put the chicken in the oven.

4 What do I _____ to do to enter the talent show?

You must fill in this form.

5 Is this your first performance?

No, I've been an actor _____ years.

6 _____ we need to sing and dance in the show?

Yes, you do. Can you dance?

11 More than a job

VOCABULARY

1 Match the words (1–6) with (a–f) to make jobs.

1 bus
2 football
3 maths
4 pop
5 police
6 shop

a assistant
b driver
c officer
d player
e singer
f teacher

2 Choose the correct words.

1 Freya wants to be a *police officer/shop assistant*. She wants to make her city a safe place.
2 Kiera's dad was a *pop singer/football player* when he was young. He was very famous and won lots of matches with his team.
3 Dan's mum is a *shop assistant/bus driver*. She takes people around the city centre.
4 My cousin is studying at university. He wants to be a *pop singer/maths teacher* and work with small children.
5 Liam's dad is a *shop assistant/police officer* in the city centre. He works in a department store.
6 My parents are both English teachers, but I want to be a *maths teacher/pop singer*. I love music and I'd like to be famous one day.

3 Complete the sentences with these jobs.

doctor   journalist   mechanic
~~police officer~~   receptionist   waitress

1 My cousin's a *police officer*. He works at the large police station in the city centre.
2 Shane's a _____ for the *Evening Star* newspaper, but he spends half his time at a desk in the office.
3 Maria's a _____ at the new Italian restaurant in town.
4 Rafaela is a _____ at the City Plaza hotel. Her job is to help the hotel guests and answer the telephone.
5 I'm a _____ and I fix cars in a garage with my dad and brother.
6 Lauren's a _____ in the city hospital. She helps old people who are ill.

4 Match these places with the pictures.

garage   hospital   hotel   ~~office~~
police station   restaurant

1   *office*

2   _____

3   _____

4   _____

5   _____

6   _____

5 Complete the crossword.

```
        1
        |
    2
    D  J  S
        |
3   _  _  _  _  _  _
        |
4   _  _  _  _  _
        |
              5
        |     |
6   _  _  _  _  _
              |
```

Across
2 people who play music on the radio or at discos
3 someone whose job is to paint things such as walls or doors
4 someone who does paintings or drawings
6 someone who cleans houses, offices or other public places

Down
1 a woman who works in business
5 someone who cooks for people in a restaurant

6 Complete the sentences with these words.

chef ~~garage~~ hospital journalist office receptionist

1 Where's Mum's car?
It's in the _garage_ . It's got a problem with the engine.
2 Is your brother a waiter in a restaurant?
No, he's the _____ . He makes the food.
3 Where's Dad?
He's talking to the hotel _____ . He wants to change our room.
4 I didn't know Sam worked in a _____ .
Yes, he's a doctor. He's just finished medicine at university.
5 What job do you want when you're older?
I don't know, but something outside. I couldn't work in an _____ all day.
6 You're very good at writing stories, Amy. You should be a _____ .
Do you think so? I'd love to work for a newspaper.

7 Match the sentence beginnings (1–6) with the endings (A–F).

1 Martin's uncle is the _D_
2 Lucy enjoys being part of _____
3 A good way to earn _____
4 I've got time _____
5 Georgina and Tom work _____
6 Isobel wants to get a _____

A money is to get a summer job.
B good job when she finishes university.
C hard in the restaurant, but they enjoy it.
D boss of the company.
E off today because I worked all weekend.
F a team in her new job.

8 Choose the correct words.

Hi, Jason

I've found a great 1) *job*/*work* for the summer. I'm going to be a 2) *waitress*/*waiter* in a beach café! It's my aunt's café, so I hope she won't make me work too 3) *hard*/*difficult*! I'll be 4) *piece*/*part* of a team of five waiters and we're all the same age, so I think it will be lots of fun. I won't 5) *do*/*earn* lots of money, but I will be next to the beach all summer. We'll get an hour 6) *off*/*over* for lunch so I plan to go swimming every day.

Anyway, how about you? Have you got a 7) *good*/*well* job for the summer?

Simon

GRAMMAR
Zero conditional

1 Match the sentence beginnings (1–6) with the endings (A–F).

1 The chef is happy _B_
2 If I work Saturday and Sunday, _____
3 If the shop is very busy, _____
4 My boss is always unhappy _____
5 If I feel very ill, _____
6 Teachers are pleased _____

A the shop assistants work more hours.
B if everyone in the restaurant enjoys their food.
C I go to the doctor.
D if all their students do their homework.
E if anyone arrives at work late.
F I always get Monday off.

2 Complete the zero conditional sentences. Use the correct form of the verbs in brackets.

1 We _____work_____ (work) quietly if the boss _____is_____ (be) in the office.
2 Rachel _____ (get) extra money if she _____ (sell) a lot of clothes.
3 If he _____ (have) time off, Jacob _____ (like) to go surfing.
4 I always _____ (feel) nervous if I _____ (have) an exam.
5 If it _____ (rain), we _____ (work) inside.
6 Sean _____ (earn) more money if he _____ (work) on Sundays.

First conditional

3 Put the words in the correct order to make sentences.

1 he'll pass / If / his exams / hard, / he studies / .
   If he studies hard, he'll pass his exams.
2 a mechanic / at his dad's garage / he becomes / if / Simon will work / .
   _____
3 angry / we don't finish / Our boss will be / our work / if / .
   _____
4 she'll be / a job at the hospital, / Danielle gets / If / part of a big team / .
   _____
5 if / a famous pop singer / a lot of records / Grace will be / she sells / .
   _____
6 you want / you'll have to / to leave work early, / If / ask the boss / .
   _____

4 Choose the correct words.

1 If I _have_/'ll have time, I'll go swimming after work.
2 William won't be late if he 'll leave/_leaves_ now.
3 If Gabrielle _works_/will work hard, she will earn more money.
4 Mark's boss will be angry if he _'s_/will be late again.
5 If I earn enough money, I buy/_'ll buy_ some new trainers.
6 The party is/_will be_ inside if the weather is bad.

5 Complete the first conditional sentences. Use the correct form of the verbs in brackets.

1 If we _____go_____ (go) now, we _____'ll get_____ (get) to the restaurant on time.
2 They _____ (put) the tables outside the café if it _____ (be) sunny.
3 You _____ (be) hungry at work if you _____ (not have) some food now.
4 My boss _____ (phone) me if I _____ (need) to work tomorrow.
5 If you _____ (like) working in a team, you _____ (love) the job at the fairground.
6 If I _____ (get) this job, I _____ (be) really happy.

Conditional with *could*

6 Make conditional sentences with *could*.

1 you / like / helping people → you / work in a hospital

   If you like helping people, you could work in a hospital.

2 she / study / hard → go / to university

3 you / like / cooking → be / a chef

4 he / enjoy / working with cars → be / a mechanic

5 Andrea / sing / well → win / the competition

6 Dan / work / hard → get / a better job

7 Complete the conditional sentences. Use the correct form of the verbs in brackets.

Ways to work or study better

Make sure you take regular breaks and get some fresh air. If you
1) _____feel_____ (feel) tired, you
2) _____ (not work) as well.
Also, if you 3) _____ (not drink) enough, you 4) _____ (have) less energy. It's a good idea to have a bottle of water on your desk.

Are you sitting at a tidy desk? If your desk 5) _____ (be) untidy, you 6) _____ (lose) things. Also, think about what you want to do each day. If you 7) _____ (make) a list, you 8) _____ (remember) what you need to do.

8 Complete the text with these words.

> babysit   earn   have to   if   'll   won't   will

Hi, Matt,

I need your help – I'm confused! I want a part-time job, but I don't know which one to choose. My neighbour has asked me to do some babysitting. 1) ____If____ I babysit in the evenings, the children 2) _____ be asleep, so it could be an easy job. I'll 3) _____ money for watching TV! If I 4) _____ at the weekends, though, I 5) _____ see my friends.

The other job is delivering newspapers. If I get this job, I'll 6) _____ get up early. I'll have to deliver the papers before 8 a.m.! But if I take this job, I 7) _____ be free all weekend.

Which job do you think I should take?

Brett

12 Summer fun!

VOCABULARY

1 **Find and write six things that you could take on holiday with you.**

s	f	l	a	p	f	l	o	p	s
u	l	r	u	c	k	s	a	c	k
m	i	v	y	n	e	u	k	l	a
a	p	g	l	a	s	n	u	f	s
c	f	u	m	a	r	g	o	l	e
a	l	a	r	m	c	l	o	c	k
f	o	l	p	h	s	a	l	e	a
l	p	i	t	u	s	s	o	c	n
i	s	p	e	r	d	s	e	d	o
d	s	u	n	c	r	e	a	m	a
t	i	n	t	n	u	s	l	a	r

1 *alarm clock*
2 ....
3 ....
4 ....
5 ....
6 ....

2 **Choose the correct words.**

1 Where's your *sun cream/alarm clock*? We need to wake up early in the morning.
2 I can't put anything else in my *rucksack/tent*. It's too heavy and it's hurting my back.
3 You're very red. Did you forget to put *flip-flops/sun cream* on?
4 Why are you wearing *sunglasses/an alarm clock*? We're inside a café!
5 There's a hole in my *tent/rucksack*. The rain is coming inside. I can feel it on my head.
6 These *flip-flops/tents* are really old. I can't walk very well in them.

3 **Complete the sentences with these words.**

> campsite ~~festival~~ map passport
> picnic suitcase

1 There's a great music ___*festival*___ in my city every June.
2 You'll need to show your _____ at the airport.
3 Is this your _____? It's very heavy! What's inside it?
4 It's a big _____ with space for 200 tents.
5 Here is our hotel on the _____. It's that black square next to the road.
6 It's a great day for a _____. Let's have lunch on the beach.

4 **Complete the table with these words and phrases.**

> ~~an accident~~ at a friend's house camping
> fun on a campsite on holiday

have	*an accident*
go	
stay	

5 Choose the correct answer, A, B or C.

1 Did you _____ a good holiday, Tim?
   A stay   (B) have   C go

2 Paul and Jack aren't here. They _____ to the beach.
   A 've stayed   B 've had   C 've gone

3 Are you _____ in the same hotel as us?
   A staying   B going   C having

4 Would you like to _____ a picnic with us?
   A go   B stay   C have

5 We _____ to an amazing kite festival in Germany.
   A had   B went   C stayed

6 Thank you for showing us round the city. We _____ a great time!
   A 've stayed   B 've gone   C 've had

7 We _____ in the same apartment on the beach every year.
   A stay   B have   C go

8 This is the fifth barbecue we _____ since we arrived!
   A 've stayed   B 've had   C 've gone

6 Complete the conversation with the correct form of *have*, *go* or *stay*.

Ben: Hi, Rosie. How are you?

Rosie: Hi, Ben. Great, thanks. I've just come back from holiday.

Ben: Really? Where did you go?

Rosie: France. We 1) _*went*_ on holiday there for two weeks. We 2) _____ a great time.

Ben: Did you go camping?

Rosie: No, we 3) _____ in a really nice apartment. My bedroom had views of the sea. It was fantastic!

Ben: So what did you do there?

Rosie: Well, we 4) _____ to the beach for a swim nearly every day.

Ben: Did you go with your parents?

Rosie: Yes, but we met a really nice family and one evening we all 5) _____ a barbecue on the beach – it was really cool. Did you have a good holiday?

Ben: Yes, thanks.

Rosie: Did you 6) _____ in your uncle's hotel again?

Ben: Yes and we 7) _____ to a kite festival – some of the kites were amazing. I'll show you my photos next time I see you.

7 Complete the conversations with the correct form of these phrasal verbs.

> look for   look out   ~~put on~~
> take off   turn off   turn on

1 It's so sunny I can't read the map.
   Here you are, you can _*put on*_ my sunglasses.

2 Joe, please _____ your boots before you come in the tent!
   OK, no problem. Shall I leave them here?

3 Can you _____ the radio? I want to listen to the weather forecast.
   Good idea. If it's going to be hot, I'll go for a swim later.

4 What _____ you _____ ?
   The keys to our hotel room. They're in the rucksack somewhere.

5 _____ ! Your football nearly hit the barbecue!
   Sorry, Dad, we'll play over there.

6 _____ you _____ your mobile phone?
   Yes, I did it as soon as we got on the plane.

8 Choose the correct words.

Welcome to
Sunnyside Holiday Apartment
Information for guests

You can 1) ~~turn on~~/look out the air conditioning with the red button near the fridge. Please remember to turn the air conditioning 2) *out/off* before you leave the apartment.

In the lounge, there is information about local beaches and festivals you can 3) *stay/go* to.

Can we please ask you to 4) *put off/take off* dirty shoes before you come in the apartment.

You can 5) *have/go* a barbecue in the garden. You can find everything you need in the kitchen cupboard.

We hope you will 6) *stay/have* a great holiday and enjoy our apartment.

GRAMMAR
–ing forms and to infinitive

1 Complete the table with these words and phrases.

> agree   bored with   decide   enjoy   forget
> good at   look forward to   want

Followed by	
-ing forms	**to infinitive**
continue	
	help
interested in	try

2 Match the sentence beginnings (1–6) with the endings (A–F).

1 I love Spain. I'm looking forward to _C_
2 My aunt likes expensive hotels. She isn't interested in _____
3 Would you like _____
4 I forgot _____
5 I love surfing, but my brother doesn't enjoy _____
6 Finlay hopes _____

A to take my sunglasses on holiday.
B to go to a festival with his friends after their exams.
C visiting Madrid in June.
D doing water sports.
E to go to Brazil next summer?
F going camping with us.

3 Choose the correct words.

1 I'm not interested in <u>taking</u>/to take any photos.
2 Rose and James are looking forward to *seeing/see* their grandparents.
3 Rachel hopes *going/to go* to Italy next year.
4 Harvey's bored with *swimming/to swim* every day.
5 I'd like *buying/to buy* some new sunglasses for my holiday.
6 Annabel forgot *bringing/to bring* her flip-flops.

Present simple passive

4 Put the words in the correct order to make sentences.

1 is / in the price of the ticket / Transport / included / .
   Transport is included in the price of the ticket.
2 checked / Your bags / at the airport / are / .
   _____
3 emailed / is / Information about the apartment / to you / .
   _____
4 are / on the beach / Ice creams and cold drinks / sold / .
   _____
5 is / on your train ticket / Your seat number / printed / .
   _____
6 are / a map of the campsite when you arrive / given / You / .
   _____

5 Complete these sentences with *is* or *are*.

1 These bags _____are_____ made by local people.
2 The food _____ cooked in front of you.
3 A free drink _____ given to every hotel guest.
4 Tickets for the festival _____ sold online and in music shops.
5 The campsite _____ used by people of all ages.
6 The boat trips _____ organised by the holiday company.

6 Complete the sentences. Use the present simple passive form of the verbs in brackets.

1 The tourists _are shown_ (show) round the castle by a guide.
2 Dogs .... (not allow) on the beach.
3 The holiday apartment .... (advertise) on a holiday website.
4 Breakfast .... (not include) in the price of the room.
5 Drinks and snacks .... (sell) at the festival.
6 Our apartment .... (clean) every day.

7 Complete the text with the correct answer, A, B or C, in each space.

Hi, Tom

Only three weeks to our holiday! I'm really looking forward to 1) .... camping. My mum's paid for the campsite. The woman at the campsite says all the information 2) .... sent by post a week before. I've decided 3) .... ask for a new tent for my birthday. I'm not interested in 4) .... a really expensive one, but our family tent is so big and heavy! I've seen a great one in the shops. It's not very expensive and a rucksack is 5) .... away free with the tent. Do you want to go shopping on Saturday? I'd 6) .... to get some new trainers before the holiday. Don't forget to 7) .... your surfboard – there's a great beach near the campsite.

I hope to 8) .... you on Saturday!

Jenny

1	A go	(B) going	C gone
2	A is	B are	C be
3	A on	B to	C in
4	A got	B get	C getting
5	A given	B gives	C giving
6	A liked	B liking	C like
7	A bring	B brought	C bringing
8	A saw	B see	C seeing

8 Complete the postcard with one word in each space.

Dear Sam

Spain is great! The apartment we're staying in is really cool and we 1) ____'re____ allowed to use the swimming pool at the hotel next door. I'm quite good 2) .... speaking Spanish now and I've made some friends here. I'm going to a beach party tomorrow – I can't wait! I bought a really nice necklace today. It 3) .... made of shells. I'm going to wear it to the beach party. The town where we're staying also has a music and dance festival this weekend. The whole town 4) .... decorated with lights and looks really pretty at night. I'm really looking forward to 5) .... to the festival. I hope 6) .... go with my new friends José and Cristina.

Love

Julie

Revision Units 11 – 12

VOCABULARY

1 Choose the correct words.

1 You need to *turn on/put on* your uniform before you start work – you can't wear your own clothes.

2 Can you *put on/turn off* the lights when you leave the office, please?

3 Where's the best place to *look for/look out* a part-time job?

4 You need to *turn off/take off* any jewellery you're wearing when you work in the kitchen.

5 *Look for/Look out*! You nearly dropped all the glasses.

6 Can you *turn on/take off* the radio, please? I always like to listen to music while I'm working.

2 Match the sentences (1–6) with the sentences (A–F).

1 Mark is the hotel receptionist. _C_

2 Jenny is a journalist. ....

3 Kerry is a mechanic. ....

4 Lucas is a DJ. ....

5 Lisa is a doctor. ....

6 Ben is a chef. ....

A He cooks in a five-star restaurant in Paris.

B She fixes cars and motorbikes.

C He answers the phone and talks to guests.

D She writes in a famous newspaper.

E People pay him to play music at parties.

F She works in a hospital in Sydney.

3 Choose the correct answer, A, B or C.

1 My dad's a painter. Last week he .... an accident and fell off his ladder, but he's OK.

   A went   (B) had   C stayed

2 Last summer we .... to the beach every day. It was a great holiday.

   A went   B had   C stayed

3 If you visit Madrid you can .... in my sister's apartment. She's in the UK at the moment.

   A go   B have   C stay

4 We visited a radio station with my school. We .... a great time. I'd like to be a DJ when I'm older.

   A went   B had   C stayed

5 Do you ever .... camping? I know a great campsite near the beach.

   A go   B have   C stay

6 Where are you .... on holiday this year? We're going to Mexico.

   A going   B having   C staying

7 We were .... a barbecue at the campsite when it started to rain. We all got very wet!

   A going   B having   C staying

8 I'm .... to a music festival at the weekend. Do you want to come?

   A going   B having   C staying

4 Complete the advert with these words.

> campsite   cleaners   ~~earn~~   for   hard   part

JOBS FOR THE SUMMER

Do you want to 1) *earn* some holiday money? Are you looking 2) .... a job where you can meet other young people? Then come and work at Joe's 3) .... ! You will be 4) .... of a great team of people who work 5) .... and have fun. We are looking for waiters and waitresses, 6) .... and kitchen assistants.

     For more information call Joe on 07778826374.

GRAMMAR

1 Choose the correct words.

1 My sister is interested in *to become/becoming* a police officer when she's older.
2 Mark **want**s *to earn/earning* lots of money and have a fast car.
3 We're looking forward to *starting/start* our summer job at the campsite.
4 Kiera really enjoys *to be/being* with children. She should be a teacher.
5 I've agreed *helping/to help* my aunt and uncle at their restaurant at weekends.
6 Robert is very good at *to fix/fixing* engines. Maybe one day he'll be a mechanic.
7 Emma forgot *switching/to switch* the lights off in the office.
8 Joe and Clare are trying *to find/finding* a Saturday job.

2 Make zero or first conditional sentences. Use the correct form of the verbs in brackets and use contractions where possible.

A

What are we doing on Saturday?

If the weather 1) ___*is*___ (be) nice, we 2) _____ (have) a barbecue in the garden.

B

Going on holiday is so expensive!

It 3) _____ (not be) very expensive if you 4) _____ (stay) on a campsite.

C

Which bands are playing at the music festival and how much are tickets?

If you 5) _____ (give) me your email address, I 6) _____ (send) you some information.

3 Complete the sentences with the present passive form of the verbs in brackets.

1 The offices ___*are cleaned*___ (clean) every afternoon.
2 You _____ (give) a uniform before you start the job.
3 The job _____ (advertise) on the Internet.
4 Emma _____ (not allow) to wear trainers at work.
5 Robots _____ (use) in my dad's factory.
6 The menu _____ (write) on a blackboard outside the café.

4 Choose the correct words.

1 If we *'ll stay/stay* in Rome, we'll visit the Colosseum.
2 You won't get burnt if you *'ll wear/wear* sun cream.
3 If you like camping, you *borrowed/could borrow* my tent.
4 If Jon and Rosie *will go/go* to Greece in July, it will be very hot.
5 I'll bring my swimsuit if we *go/'ll go* to the beach.
6 James won't go on the school trip if he *doesn't get/won't get* a passport.

Pearson Education Limited
Edinburgh Gate
Harlow
Essex CM20 2JE
England
and Associated Companies throughout the world.

www.pearsonelt.com

First published 2014
Ninth impression 2019

ISBN: 978-1-4479-1389-4

Set in 10pt Mixage ITC Std
Printed in Slovakia by Neografia

The publisher would like to thank the following for their kind
permission to reproduce their photographs:

(Key: b-bottom; c-centre; l-left; r-right; t-top)

Alamy Images: Alvey & Towers Picture Library 33, C-images 31t,
doughoughton 28br, geogphotos 28tr, Germany 29tl, imac 34tl,
Imagemore Ltd 18 (3), Justin Kase z12z 31br, Mar Photographics
34tr; **Corbis:** moodboard 34cl; **DK Images:** Frank Greenaway 17;
Fotolia.com: bennyartist 57, bloomua 18 (1), chrisdorney 18 (5), Brian
Jackson 18 (2), monticellllo 16, photog45 28bl, Rbut 63; **Getty Images:**
American Idol 2012 / FOX 46, Photographer's Choice 30, Purestock
37, Roy Rainford / Robert Harding 41, X Factor / Ray Mickshaw / Fox
45; **PhotoDisc:** Life File / Andrew Ward 27; **Shutterstock.com:** Lilac
Mountain 29tr, Taina Sohlman 28tl, tankist276 34cr, Tupungato 18 (4),
wheatley 31bl; **SuperStock:** Cultura Limited 34br, Ian Murray / Loop
Images 25, Tetra Images 34bl, Travelshots 61

Cover images: *Front:* **Shutterstock.com:** Petrenko Andriy

All other images © Pearson Education

Every effort has been made to trace the copyright holders and we
apologise in advance for any unintentional omissions. We would be
pleased to insert the appropriate acknowledgement in any subsequent
edition of this publication.